SPEAKING OF ART

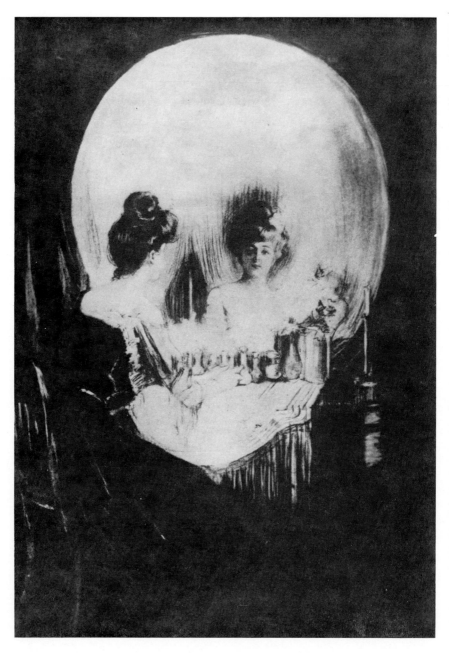

Charles Allan Gilbert (1873-1929)

All Is Vanity

SPEAKING OF ART

by

PETER KIVY

MARTINUS NIJHOFF / THE HAGUE / 1973

ISBN 90 247 1491 5

15- 514/5
PRINTED IN THE NETHERLANDS

CONTENTS

PREFACE

As the title of this book was meant to suggest, its subject is the way we talk about (and write about) works of art: or, rather, *one* of the *ways*, namely, the way we *describe* works of art for critical purposes. Because I wished to restrict my subject matter in this way, I have made a sharp, and no doubt largely artificial distinction between *describing* and *evaluating*. And I must, at the outset, guard against a misreading of this distinction to which I have left myself open.

In distinguishing between evaluative and descriptive aesthetic judgments, I am *not* saying that when I assert "X is *p*," where *p* is a "descriptive" term like "unified," or "delicate," or "garish," I may not at the same time be evaluating X too; and I am *not* saying that when I make the obviously "evaluative" assertion "X is good," I may not be describing X. Clearly, if I say "X is unified" I am evaluating X in that unity is a good-making feature of works of art; and as it is correct in English at least to call an evaluation a description, I do not want to suggest that if an assertion is evaluative, it cannot be descriptive (although there have been many philosophers who have thought this indeed to be the case). All that I shall mean, throughout this study, by a descriptive aesthetic judgment is one that does not commit the judger to the further judgment that the work of art about which the first judgment was made is "aesthetically good" or "aesthetically bad" (or anything synonymous with either). And all that I shall mean by an evaluative aesthetic judgment is the outright assertion "X is aesthetically good" or "X is aesthetically bad" (or anything synonymous with either). Thus I am using "evaluative" and "descriptive" in special senses which they do not ordinarily have. This has been done for convenience of expression only, and is not a commitment to any philosophical theory about the evaluative-descriptive distinction.

Our subject, then, is aesthetic descriptions, in the special sense explained above, our thesis that aesthetic describing is logically of a piece with other descriptive discourse in ordinary language. In the first chapter, I have attempted to spell out what that logic is. In the second, I have tried to show that the exercise of "taste" in aesthetic judgment is not incompatible with the logic ascribed to aesthetic descriptions. The third chapter is devoted to a refutation of the claim that the behavior of descriptive aesthetic terms is markedly different from the behavior of nonaesthetic descriptive terms. This theme is developed further in Chapter IV, which is concerned with the question of whether the distinction between being and appearing has any place in aesthetic describing. (The conclusion is that it has.) In the penultimate chapter, the question is raised whether aesthetic descriptions are descriptions of "qualities" or "aspects"; and it is argued that whether they are the one or the other, their logic will not be appreciably different than the model outlined in Chapter I. Finally, the topic of "aesthetic objectivity" is broached, and the conclusion reached that the degree of "objectivity" allowed to aesthetic terms throughout this study is not incompatible with either our attitudes towards, or our conduct of aesthetic disputes.

There is an old bit of advice to the author to the effect that he must never say in the beginning of his book what he intends to do in the rest of it, in case he does not succeed in doing what he sets out to do. Clearly, I have disregarded this anonymous counsel in my own preface. But I have been the beneficiary of far more valuable advice which I have not so completely ignored, and which it is both my duty and my pleasure to keep from being anonymous. I am profoundly grateful to Arthur C. Danto, Elmer H. Duncan, Lindley Hanlon, Ronald Munson, Miriam Munson, Edward A. Spiegel, B. R. Tilghman, Alan Tormey, and Judith Tormey for their unselfish assistance.

Work on this book was made possible by a Faculty Fellowship from the Rutgers Research Council.

To my mother and father

"But on general grounds we may say that it cannot be the whole character of anything to seem to be something. There must be something which it is, as well as something which it seems to be."

– Sir David Ross

CHAPTER I

THE CONDITION-GOVERNED MODEL

Introduction

If X is an integer greater than one which has no factors other than itself and one, then it is a prime number. Being greater than one and having no factors other than itself and one are necessary conditions of an integer's being a prime number: no integer that is not greater than one or has factors other than itself and one can be a prime number. And being an integer greater than one and having no factors other than itself and one are also sufficient conditions for being a prime number: we need know nothing else about X except that it is an integer greater than one and has no factors other than itself and one to conclude with logical certainty that X is a prime number. "X is an integer greater than one which has no factors other than itself and one" implies "X is a prime number." And the term "prime number" is *condition-governed* in that there are logically necessary-and-sufficient conditions for any number being prime, namely, that it is an integer greater than one and that it has no factors other than itself and one.

The terms we use in our every-day discourse do not, however, behave in this way. No one can tell us, for example, the logically necessary-and-sufficient conditions for a man's being *intelligent*. Nor could we ever hope to list all of the features that might be appealed to as intelligent-making ones – not only because the list would be an extremely long one but for the more compelling reason that the intelligent-making features of the future cannot possibly be known to us now, any more than Socrates could have known that being able to understand the Special Theory of Relativity would be a mark of intelligence in the twentieth century. Thus there are no necessary-and-sufficient conditions for being intelligent; "intelligent" is not condition-governed in the sense in which "prime number" is.

But is it condition-governed at all?

Certainly there is an important respect in which "intelligent" and "prime number" are both condition-governed. If Mr. A were to deny that X is a prime number while affirming that X is an integer greater than one which has no factors other than itself and one, we would feel something very odd were taking place: most probably we would suspect that Mr. A doesn't know what "prime number" or "integer greater than one which has no factors other than itself and one" means. Likewise, if Mr. A were to deny that Mr. B is intelligent and yet assert (1) that Mr. B had been a Quiz-Kid, (2) that Mr. B understands the Special Theory of Relativity, (3) that Mr. B discovered an innoculation that prevents cancer, (4) that Mr. B is co-author of the definitive work on Babylonian mathematics, (5) that Mr. B is proficient in fifteen languages, we would surely suspect that something every bit as odd were afoot as in the case of Mr. A asserting "X is an integer greater than one which has no factors other than itself and one" and denying "X is a prime number." We would want to say, "If (1) through (5) are a true description of Mr. B, then we are simply not free to deny that Mr. B is intelligent." We would want to say that (1) through (5) together imply the further statement "Mr. B is intelligent" (although we could deny any one of the five without denying "Mr. B is intelligent," whereas we could not deny either "X is an integer greater than one" or "X has no factors other than itself and one" and still assert "X is a prime number").[1] We would be likely to say that Mr. A did not really know what "intelligent" means if he asserted (1) through (5) and denied "Mr. B is intelligent," just as we would be likely to claim that he did not understand the meaning of "prime number" if he asserted "X is an integer greater than one and has no factors other than itself and one " and denied "X is a prime number."

We shall therefore want to say that there is a second kind of condition-governed term for which words like "intelligent" are paradigm cases. Throughout this book it will always be this second kind of condition-governed term that we have in mind when we speak of the condition-governed model.

But before we proceed we must distinguish yet another kind of condition-governed term which will play a prominent role: the kind exemplified by "red" and other color words. And it will be useful, in

---

[1] See, for example, Hugo Meynell, "On the Foundations of Aesthetics," *The British Journal of Aesthetics*, VIII (1968), p. 18, and John Wisdom, "Metaphysics and Verification," reprinted in *Philosophy and Psychoanalysis* (Oxford: Basil Blackwell, 1964), pp. 82–83.

this connection, to distinguish as well among what Stephen Toulmin calls "complex," "simple," and "scientific" qualities.[2]

The word "intelligent" names a complex quality: complex in that we can analyze it; break it down into components. An intelligent man is intelligent in virtue of his possessing certain other properties: for example, the ability to play chess, to do mathematics, to read foreign languages, and the like. But the word "red" in every-day life names a simple quality: simple because unanalyzable. We do not, in ordinary discourse, say that a fire engine is red in virtue of its possessing other properties. We simply see that it is red and cannot appeal to other properties in pointing out its redness to someone else. There are, however, instances in which "red," for example, names a complex quality; these instances come up in scientific discourse. We might say that a certain luminous body is red in virtue of its emitting energy between some given range of wave lengths. In this case, "red" is the name of a complex analyzable property not perceived in the way we perceive the redness of the fire engine. "Red," here, is the name of a scientific quality, scientific qualities being a sub-set of the class of complex qualities – those, namely, that are analyzable because they figure in some scientific theory or other.

If we now ask whether "red" is a condition-governed term, a difficulty arises. Frank Sibley, an author about whom we will have much to say as we proceed, thinks of color terms as paradigmatically *non*-condition-governed:

some ... sorts of concepts are ... not condition-governed. We do not apply simple color words by following rules or in accordance with principles. We see that the book is red by looking. ...[3]

Yet a recent critic of Sibley, J. Williamson, finds this contention at least arguable, if not a downright howler:

do we not follow any rule about "puce"? None at all? Might we not say that a man who sincerely said that grass is puce was off the rails?[4]

And Isabel Hungerland, another author who will figure prominently in what follows, takes the exact opposite view from Sibley's with regard

[2] Stephen Toulmin, *Reason in Ethics* (Cambridge: Cambridge University Press, 1968), pp. 10–18.
[3] Frank Sibley, "Aesthetic Concepts," reprinted in *Philosophy Looks at the Arts*, ed. Joseph Margolis (New York: Charles Scribner's Sons, 1962), p. 77.
[4] J. Williamson (in a review of *Philosophy Looks at the Arts*), *Australasian Journal of Philosophy*, XLI (1963), p. 439.

to color terms, using them as paradigm cases of the condition-governed.[5]

Part of the confusion here can be cleared up by keeping in mind the difference between "red" when it is used to name a simple quality (in ordinary discourse) and when it is used to name a scientific one (in some technical language). For "red" when used to name a scientific quality is, clearly, condition-governed, and condition-governed, as a matter of fact, in the strongest way. Emitting energy within a certain specifiable range of wave lengths is a necessary-and-sufficient condition for being red in the scientific context. But when "red" is used in ordinary discourse, it is condition-governed in neither the first nor the second way. For it names a simple quality that cannot be reduced to more basic components. There are no other features of an object besides its redness that we can appeal to in pointing out to someone that it is red. It is the ordinary, non-technical use of "red," clearly, that Sibley has in mind; and he is quite right in insisting that "red," used in this way, is not condition-governed in the manner of terms like "prime" or "intelligent."

But this is not all there is to say in the matter. For neither Mr. Williamson nor Mrs. Hungerland seems to have scientific qualities in mind. So our difficulty remains: Sibley says that "red" is non-condition-governed in ordinary discourse; Williamson and Hungerland deny it; and appearances cannot be saved by claiming that Sibley is using "red" in a different way than are Williamson and Hungerland. "Red," then, as Sibley, Williamson and Hungerland are using the term, is the name of a simple quality; hence we cannot appeal to any other property besides redness itself in supporting the assertion "X is red." And if "red" *were* condition-governed, as Williamson and Hungerland seem to claim, we would be able to do this. Are Mr. Williamson and Mrs. Hungerland simply in error?

It is at this point that we must introduce a *third* kind of condition-governed term, somewhat different from the other two. If Mr. A were to say "X is red" and Mr. B were to say "X is blue," there are two very obvious moves that could be made towards resolving the disagreement: (1) Mr. A (or Mr. B) might suggest (for example) that X be viewed in direct sunlight rather than artificial light; or (2) Mr. A (or Mr. B) might suggest that Mr. B (or Mr. A)"have his eyes examined." In the first case the viewing conditions are in question, in the second case

---

[5] Isabel C. Hungerland, "The Logic of Aesthetic Concepts," *Proceedings and Addresses of the American Philosophical Association*, XXXVI (1962–63), pp. 43–66, *passim.*

the state of the viewer's perceptual faculties. In other words, even when "red" is used in ordinary discourse, as the name of a simple quality, normal conditions of perception and perceiver play some part in determining whether or not X is really red. And in this manner "red" and other color words are condition-governed. But the manner is a different one from either of the first two as there are no properties or features of X other than its redness in virtue of which it is red. Nevertheless, normal conditions of perception and perceiver "govern" color terms in a way. So we shall say that "red" and other color words are condition-governed, making sure always to distinguish this kind of condition-governed term from the previous two.

We have, then, three ways in which a term can be condition-governed: the strong way in which "prime number" is condition-governed; (2) the looser way in which "intelligent" is condition-governed; and (3) the altogether different way in which "red" is condition-governed in virtue of there being normal conditions of perception and perceiver.

This book is concerned with the terms we use to describe works of art for critical purposes. As the argument progresses, the delineation of this now rather dimly outlined class will bit by bit become more distinct. But it is time now to state and begin to defend our major thesis which is that these terms we use to describe works of art are condition-governed in the second way; the way for which words like "intelligent" provide the paradigm. The remainder of the present chapter will be devoted to defending this thesis by exhibiting the conditions that govern the term "unity" as it is applied in musical contexts.

Unity in Music: A Test Case

There is a very familiar sense in which music is said to be "unified"; and I think it can best be introduced with an example. I quote from a well-known study of Beethoven's string quartets:

> The second violin murmurs the second theme, a suave and consoling melody based on the second phrase ... of the first theme. ...
>   In this passage the *Allegro* thus gains a unity of inspiration.
> . . . .
>   The *Menuetto* opens with the identical notes that open the *Allegro*, thus at once adding to the sense of unity in the conception of the work. ...[6]

---

[6] Joseph de Marliave, *Beethoven's Quartets*, trans. Hilda Andrews (New York: Dover Publications, 1961), pp. 24–27.

Unity is ascribed here in virtue of a musical work or fragment possessing what I shall hereafter call (rather loosely) "monothematic structure." There are, of course, a great many compositional techniques for which such a phrase might be appropiate. But in general what is meant by a monothematic structure is one in which some theme, fragment of a theme, rhythmic figure, harmonic progression, or even a single chord (the "Tristan" chord, for instance) is introduced at various points throughout a musical work, or part of a musical work, so that its introduction either sets up a pattern of repetition (as, say, in the baroque *ritornello* or the classical rondo) or forms the material out of which fresh musical ideas arise (as, for example, in the theme-and-variation, monothematic sonata movement, twelve-tone and serial techniques, and so forth).

There *seems*, however, to be a second sense of "unified" in which unity is ascribed to a musical composition even though monothematic structure is known to be absent. And again I think this can best be illustrated with an example. The last notes of Verdi's *Stabat Mater*, Tovey writes,

are those to which the three words "Stabat Mater dolorosa" are set at the beginning; otherwise there is no theme to hold the work together. His [Verdi's] enormous talent for composition . . . enables him to make the lines of the poem roll on in their groups of three like a planet in its orbit.[7]

I want to gloss this passage as follows: In spite of its obvious lack of unity ("no theme to hold the work together") Verdi's *Stabat Mater* appears unified ("like a planet in its orbit"). What I am suggesting, then, is that we do *not* have here two senses of the term "unified," one synonymous with "monothematic" and the other not, but, rather, in the first instance, a case of being unified and in the second a case of only *seeming* so (albeit expressed in a highly metaphoric way). I am suggesting that the best way to describe this aesthetic situation is in the language of *being* and *appearing*, understanding that this is one of those cases in which, as Harold Osborne puts it, "We . . . see things otherwise than they are without believing or tending to believe that they are as we see them."[8] That is to say, Verdi's *Stabat Mater* does not cease to appear unified when we discover it is not really unified, just as the stick in water appears bent even after we discover, by feeling with our hands, that it is not really bent.

[7] Donald Francis Tovey, *Essays in Musical Analysis* (London: Oxford University Press, 1935–39), vol.VI, p. 58.
[8] Harold Osborne, "On Artistic Illusion," *The British Journal of Aesthetics*, IX (1969), p. 12.

We sometimes say that a rose appears pink although it really is not. Likewise, we can say that in our second example the *Stabat Mater* appears unified although it is not. The opposite case, of course, would be of a rose that is pink but appears not to be. And to fill out the scheme, I want to adduce a corresponding example of musical unity and its apparent absence. I quote now from Sir George Grove's discussion of Beethoven's *Eroica* and its early performing history.

The first report of the music ... is in the Vienna letter of the *Allgemeine musi-kalische Zeitung*, for February 13, 1805. ... the correspondent describes it "as virtually a daring, wild fantasia of inordinate length and extreme difficulty of execution." ...
The report of the performance of April, 1805 ... is even more unfavorable. The writer finds no reason to modify his former judgment. "No doubt the work displays bold and great ideas, and that vast power of expression which is the property of the composer; but there can also be no doubt that it would gain immensely if Beethoven would consent to shorten it (it lasts a full hour) and introduce more light, clearness, and unity. ..." Allowance must be made for those who were hearing so original a work for the first time; but the accusation of want of unity is strange when one remembers the persistent way in which characteristic portions of the principal subjects of each movement keep recurring – no less than thirty-seven times in the first *Allegro*, for instance. Judging by one's present feelings and the evidence of fact, it is the last blame that could be urged.[9]

The surprise which Grove evinces towards denial of unity clearly indicates that *he* is using the term very much in the way I have suggested prevails among musicians and those who write about music. Monothematic structure ("the persistent way in which the characteristic portions of the principal subjects of each movement keep recurring") Grove takes to be sufficient for the ascription of unity; and since the first Allegro of the *Eroica* manifestly exhibits such structure, he finds it odd that its unity should be denied. But, as Grove insists, "Allowance must be made for those who were hearing so original a work for the first time." And what Grove is asking us to make allowance for, clearly, is the contemporary listener's inability to hear the monothematic structure. *If* he had heard it, Grove suggests, he could not possibly have denied unity to the *Eroica*, for that is what having unity means. The work *appeared* chaotic because the monothematic structure was not heard.

Indeed there is very good reason to believe that this early reviewer did not, in fact, perceive the monothematic structure of the first

---

[9] George Grove, *Beethoven and His Nine Symphonies* (New York: Dover Publications, 1962), pp. 89–90.

Allegro (say) at all. By his own admission it lacked "clearness," and this is not surprising. As clear as it was to Grove in 1896, and to us today, the *Eroica* was understandably opaque to the listener in 1805. Consider what an impression Beethoven's Third Symphony must have made on an audience that was still assimilating late Haydn and Mozart and Beethoven's own disturbing early works. For the *Eroica* is probably the paradigm case of the bold innovative stroke in music: "One of the incomprehensible deeds in arts and letters, the greatest single step made by an individual composer in the history of the symphony and in the history of music in general."[10] Surely it is not surprising that the first impression of the *Eroica* was chaos although there is hardly a finer example of symphonic organization in the literature. Less complex "objects" have required long and close scrutiny before they gave up their secrets. It is hardly inconceivable that two (probably bad) performances of the Third Symphony in 1805 failed to reveal its monothematic structure even to a sympathetic listener.

There is, however, no way of proving that the correspondent of 1805 did not hear the monothematic structure of Beethoven's *Eroica* – that is, was not aware of it. All we can say with any kind of assurance is that there is nothing implausible about his not having heard it. Yet he may have heard and been aware of it for all of that. So we are really faced here with two "hypotheses" which account equally well for the correspondent's report. We can say that he did indeed hear the monothematic structure and hence was using "unified" in a quite different sense than the one in which Grove was using the term. Or we can say that he did not hear it, that the *Eroica* appeared to him to lack unity, that he felt no cause to doubt its lack of unity, and hence that he mistakenly declared it disunified.

But suppose we opt for the former hypothesis. Suppose we say that there is more than one sense – that there are perhaps many senses – of musically "unified." If we do, we will find grave problems in trying to spell out this other sense, or these other senses. For there seems to be only one hard-core sense of "unified" in musical discourse: and that is "monothematic." It is not as if we can say "unified" means either "monothematic" or . . . , and fill in the blank with anything that can account for the cases in which unity is ascribed in the absence of monothematic structure, or denied in its presence. And this has driven some to con-

[10] Paul Henry Lang, *Music in Western Civilization* (New York: W. W. Norton, 1941), p. 763.

clude that therefore the term is non-condition-governed. What I am suggesting is that we simply opt for the latter hypothesis, which can account equally well for the facts of aesthetic discourse and perhaps strike a less paradoxical note into the bargain. "The most intelligible way of speaking of it seems to be this."[11]

To sum up, then, I am arguing that we can best understand the various ascriptions of unity to music in terms of what *is* and what *appears*. And I have exhibited three musical examples which correspond, I am claiming, to three possible cases of being and appearing: being p and appearing p; being not-p and appearing p; being p and appearing not-p. Now all of this has been presented, I realize, in rather bald and dogmatic fashion. So what I want now to do is further explore this position by fortifying it against three possible objections.

Refutations and Rejoinders

(1) The first objection is a variation on the two-hundred-year-old theme, to be discussed in more general terms in a succeeding chapter, that in aesthetic perception we are interested only in the way things *appear*. Along such lines, one might argue that it makes no sense to talk about the Beethoven quartet *being* unified and Verdi's *Stabat Mater* only *appearing* so; for from the aesthetic point of view the appearance is all that counts, and to appear unified is, from the aesthetic point of view, to be unified.

Now there are at least two possible kinds of conditions – what H. P. Grice calls "doubt or denial" conditions[12] – under which one might remark that a work of art *seemed* or *appeared* to have some quality. One might, in the first place, believe that a work of art is p, and yet have some reason not to be sure: if, for example, one were perceiving it for the first time and felt that further acquaintance might reveal new features relevant to the judgment. This may be the attitude we feel should have been taken by the early reviewer of Beethoven's *Eroica*. But critics of the arts have not been known for the modesty of their pronouncements. (In fact I once heard a highly respected American composer and critic say that he had never made a mistaken judgment in his life about a musical composition!)

[11] Joseph Butler, *Five Sermons* (New York: Bobbs-Merrill, 1950), p. 57 (Sermon XI, "Upon the Love of Our Neighbour").
[12] H. P. Grice, "The Causal Theory of Perception," reprinted in *Perceiving, Sensing, and Knowing*, ed. Robert J. Swartz (Garden City: Doubleday Anchor Books, 1965), pp. 440–44.

In the second place, one might have no reason to believe that a work of art is *p*, but say that it *seems* or *appears p* in the same way that one says that the stick in water seems or appears bent even though knowing that it is not. Instances of both kinds abound in discourse about the arts; and the term "unified" provides its share of examples.

Let us begin with the former. They are easy to find. Here follow two very obvious cases of statements made under "doubt" conditions: conditions under which one has some reason to advance a judgment only tentatively, and without assurance of its correctness:

The most interesting thing on the program of last Thursday night's Philharmonic concert in Philharmonic Hall was a performance, apparently the first ever heard here, of Scriabin's Second Symphony. ... It is long, it is diffuse, *it sometimes does not seem to be going anywhere in particular.*

The Brubeck work was preceded on the program by Carl Nielsen's Fourth Symphony, *which to me sounded* noisy and *incoherent.*[13]

Under the assumption that to be "unified" or "coherent" is simply to appear (or seem) "unified" or "coherent," and vice versa, we can interpret the assertion "Nielsen's Fourth is incoherent" as "Nielsen's Fourth sounds (or seems) incoherent." What, then, are we to say of an obviously qualified assertion like "Nielsen's Fourth sounds (or seems) incoherent to me"? Clearly this suggests doubt. But doubt about *what*? If I say the rose appears pink, in certain contexts, I express doubt about whether it really is pink. If I say "Nielsen's Fourth sounded incoherent to me," what am I expressing doubt about? About how it really *sounded* (if that makes sense)? Are we to understand it as "Nielsen's Fourth seemed to sound incoherent to me"? That clearly will not do. If it is not nonsense, then to say "Nielsen's Fourth seemed to sound incoherent to me" is to express doubt about how it really sounded, just as to say "The rose seems to me to appear pink," if *that* is not nonsense, is to express doubt that the rose really appears pink. But our reviewer gives no evidence of expressing doubt about how Nielsen's Fourth appeared to him; it appeared incoherent.

Perhaps, then, the following will be preferable: "Nielsen's Fourth sounded incoherent to me" can be understood to mean "Nielsen's Fourth sounded incoherent to me at the last performance but will sound coherent when I become more accustomed to it." But suppose I ask why it will not continue to appear incoherent? The most obvious

[13] Winthrop Sargeant, in *The New Yorker*, XLV (1969), No. 9 (p. 167) and No. 14 (p. 138).

answer is: "Because it isn't really incoherent." Or maybe: "Because incoherent music always begins to seem coherent when you get used to it.' Or just: "Because music always begins to seem coherent when you get used to it." In all three cases, however, that Nielsen's Fourth *really is* something – coherent in the first case, incoherent in the second, and not coherent in the third – is assumed in the statement that it will not continue to appear as it appeared. We might say, to try yet another tack, that "Nielsen's Fourth sounded incoherent to me" (with emphasis on the *to me*) is meant to express doubt about how it sounded to others, in which case we could read it as "Nielsen's Fourth sounded incoherent *to me*, but perhaps it sounded coherent *to you*." Again, though, the force of the statement is to express doubt about the coherence or incoherence of Nielsen's Fourth. To say "X seems *p* to me, but perhaps it doesn't seem *p* to you," is to initiate a discussion of whether X really is *p*; to ask if it seemed the same to you is to ask for confirmation (or disconfirmation). What is doubtful, ultimately, is whether X really is *p*, not how it appears. All of which is simply to say that in all discourse, including aesthetic, the distinction between being and appearing is assumed in the use of the word "appear."

I want now to turn to the second kind of condition under which one might say that a work of art appears rather than is unified, the "denial" condition, the situation in which one knows that the object is not as it appears.

There is a quip, sometimes attributed to Mark Twain, that "Wagner's music is better than it sounds." It would be equally odd, I presume, to say "Wagner's music sounds better than it is." But would it be odd to say "Wagner's music sounds more *unified* than it is"? Is this nonsense in the way that the first two statements surely are? If so, then it must be nonsense as well to interpret Tovey as saying that "Verdi's *Stabat Mater* sounds more unified than it is" – which is exactly the interpretation of Tovey that I am suggesting we make.

Well what exactly is odd about saying "Wagner's music sounds better than it is"? Is there anything odd, for example, in saying "This rose appears redder than it is"? Let us interpret each assertion in two ways:

(a) Wagner's music sometimes sounds better than it is.
(b) Wagner's music always (under all conceivable conditions) sounds better than it is.
(c) This rose sometimes looks redder than it is.

(d) This rose always (under all conceivable conditions) looks redder than it is.

What emerges from this breakdown, I think, is that (a) and (b) are *both* odd; whereas (c) is not odd but (d) is. It would certainly be odd to say in ordinary, non-technical discourse, "This rose always (under all conceivable conditions) looks redder than it is." That certainly is bordering on nonsense, because *part* of what we mean, in ordinary discourse, by "being red" is that the rose appears red under at least *some* conceivable condition. It would not be odd, however, to say "This rose sometimes looks redder than it is." It may look redder at sunset, or sunrise, or at some other time when the lighting is unusual. But it is just as odd to say "Wagner's music sometimes sounds better than it is" as it is to say "Wagner's music always sounds better than it is." There just does not seem to be any context in which the former assertion makes sense. Wagner's music could never have sounded better than it is.

What, now, of the assertion "Verdi's *Stabat Mater* sounds more unified than it is"? Let us interpret it, like the others, in two ways:
(e) Verdi's *Stabat Mater* sometimes sounds more unified than it is.
(f) Verdi's *Stabat Mater* always (under all conceivable conditions) sounds more unified than it is.

If it makes no sense to assert (e) – if (e) has the same status as (a) – the proposed treatment of unity will fail. I want to claim, on the contrary, that (e) has the same status as (c), and that (f) has the same status as (d). It does make sense to assert "Verdi's *Stabat Mater* sometimes sounds more unified than it is," and, when properly construed, it does not make sense to assert "Verdi's *Stabat Mater* always (under all conceivable conditions) sounds more unified than it is." In other words, "Verdi's *Stabat Mater* sounds more unified than it is" corresponds to "This rose appears redder than it is," and not to "Wagner's music sounds better than it is."

We distinguished previously two cases in which someone might say something *appeared* so-and-so: the first, in which it is not known, and the second, in which it is known that what appears is not as it appears. Consider the following two examples:

(i) I am standing at the foot of the Matterhorn looking up at a distant figure climbing the mountain. It appears to me to be a man in a white fur parka with a funny hat on his head. But the figure is too distant for me to be sure. So I get out my telescope and take a look. The figure turns out not to be a man at all but a mountain goat with broken antlers. I take the telescope away from my eye, look at the figure as I had before: it now looks no longer like a man; I see it as a mountain goat.

(ii) I am am looking at the so-called Müller-Lyer lines:

One appears to be longer than the other. I place a rule up against each line. The lines now appear to be the same length. I remove the rules and look at the lines as before; but try as I may, they look unequal again although I now know perfectly well that they are not.

Case (ii) I described previously as a case in which something continues to appear p even though I know it is not-p. But even case (ii) cannot be a case in which it makes sense to say: "The left line always (under all conceivable conditions) looks longer than the right line." The difference, on this regard, between case (i) and case (ii), is that after I know that the figure really is a mountain goat, it stops appearing a man and starts appearing a mountain goat, even though I view it under the same conditions as before. Whereas after I know that the Müller-Lyer lines are equal, they still appear unequal under the old conditions. I discovered that the man was really a mountain goat by changing the original viewing conditions: looking through the telescope. Similarly, I discovered that the Müller-Lyer lines are really equal by changing the original viewing conditons: placing rules simultaneously next to each line. The figure is seen to be a goat when viewed through the telescope; and the lines are seen to be equal when rules are placed beside them. However, when the original viewing conditions are restored – when the telescope and rules are removed – the figure continues to look like a mountain goat; the lines, on the contrary, do not continue to look equal. Yet the lines did, under the previous conditions at least, appear equal.

Now there are *no* conceivable conditions under which Wagner's music sounds better than it is, which is why "Wagner's music sometimes sounds better than it is" makes nonsense. And if it makes sense to say "Verdi's *Stabat Mater* sometimes sounds more unified than it is," there must be conditions conceivable under which Verdi's *Stabat Mater* sounds more unified than it is. What are these conditions?

Under what might be called "distant viewing," the *Stabat Mater* rolls along in its orbit. It is upon scrutinizing the work that we reveal to ourselves its lack of unity – "no theme to hold the work together." When we listen for thematic relationships, we do not find them. It is when we are directly aware, in our listening, of the absence of monothematic structure that the work ceases to appear unified. A "rule" has been applied. But like the Müller-Lyer lines, the *Stabat Mater* appears again in the old way when the previous conditions are restored; when we take our distance again. Like an impressionist painting, the *Stabat Mater* can be approached and receded from: at a certain distance the Verdi hangs together, giving no hint of incoherence; it is at close quarters that we discover the unity of the Beethoven quartet and the apparent unity only of the *Stabat Mater*. Nor is there any mystery of deep principle involved here. What metaphors like "distant viewing" are meant to describe is a very ordinary aspect of music appreciation: that our attention in listening can sometimes be fixed on details and sometimes on larger structures; that sometimes we listen analytically and sometimes not. I can listen to a Beethoven quartet and fix my attention on the intricate thematic relationships; or I can attend to the sensuous surface of sound. And the point is that when I listen to it analytically, it reveals a structure the *Stabat Mater* will never reveal under similar scrutiny: which is what justifies the conclusion that the quartet is really unified and the *Stabat Mater* is not.

(2) The ascription of apparent unity may seem to have paradoxical results also in the area of valuation. If an object is valued highly for (in part) being p, then discovering that it isn't p but only appears p will force it lower in our estimation. If I buy a knife because I think it is sharp, and then discover that it only looks sharp and really is not, I will certainly be disappointed. Likewise, it follows that if unity is a good-making feature of music, the discovery that a work is not unified but only appears so must reduce its aesthetic value in our eyes. If we do not agree to this, then we are not using "is" and "appears" in their normal senses. As a matter of fact, unity does seem to be a good-making feature of music. The statement "Unity is good" may indeed be analytic;[14] that is, it may be self-contradictory to assert (say) "The symphony is bad because it is unified." It follows, then, that discovering the apparent unity only of Verdi's *Stabat Mater* must make

---

[14] Elmer H. Duncan, "Arguments Used in Ethics and Aesthetics: Two Differences," *"Journal of Aesthetics and Art Criticism*, XXV (1967), p. 428. Cf. Kenneth M. Stampp, Jr., "Unity as a Necessary Condition," *Journal of Aesthetics and Art Criticism*, XXVII (1968), pp. 141–43. For reasons which escape me, Stampp claims that if "Unity is good" is analytic, then unity must be a neceessary condition for aesthetic goodness. He concludes from this that since unity is not a necessary condition for aesthetic goodness (which it certainly is not), the statement "Unity is good" cannot be analytic. But how it follows that if the statement "Unity is good" is analytic, unity must be a necessary condition for aesthetic goodness, I simply cannot make out. By accepting "Unity is good" as analytic, all we are accepting is that it is logically contradictory to say "X is bad because it is unified"; and from this it does not follow that unity is a necessary condition for aesthetic goodness.

us value it less highly than we did when we did not realize that it only appeared unified. And this, it might be argued, is contraintuitive: we do not value the *Stabat Mater* less for the fact that it does not possess monothematic structure. I want to argue that it is not at all contraintuitive.

Suppose I try to ward off an attacker by brandishing a knife. While I hold the knife I run my thumb over the edge and, to my horror, discover that it is a stage-knife with a dull edge. My evaluation of the knife, in this unpleasant situation, has been greatly altered. But it is a stage-knife, after all, and looks quite sharp. So I might still succeed in bluffing my antagonist. I am, as a matter of fact, in a better position than if the knife neither was nor looked sharp. In this particular situation I would say that a knife which looked sharp and was sharp is best, a knife which looked sharp but was not second, and a knife which neither was nor looked sharp a very poor third.

Along similar lines, musicians, music-historians, and music critics tend generally to consider monothematic structure a good-making feature and, all things being equal, value more highly music with monothematic structure than music which I described as merely *appearing* unified; and value such apparently unified music more highly than music which does not appear unified at all.

Our aesthetic case does, to be sure, present a further complication. For it may be that one of the qualities we admire in the *Stabat Mater*, namely, its great melodic spontaneity, is incompatible with real unity: with, that is, monothematic structure of any elaborate kind. And so it might seem somewhat misleading to say that we admire it less than we would if its structure were monothematic. Because if the structure were monothematic, the great melodic spontaneity which we so admire in Verdi would be lost. I think a similar point is being made in the following remark:

It is questionable whether unity as a "good making quality" could really improve Bruckner's music. Would it not, on the contrary, eliminate that sense of naive disjointed grandeur which is so essential to the Brucknerian aesthetic?[15]

In this case we might want to reply that a fair exchange is no robbery; that we *do* value Verdi's music less for lack of monothematic structure, but value it more for melodic spontaneity, and value Bruckner's music less for lack of unity but more for its "sense of naive disjointed gran-

[15] Stampp, *op. cit.*, p. 142.

deur." We add the same amount we subtract (if, that is, we value melodic spontaneity and "naive disjointed grandeur" as much as monothematic structure); and thus we do in fact value Verdi's music less for lacking monothematic structure, and Bruckner's less for lacking unity, although it may not show up in the final sum. But we do not value Verdi or Bruckner less as artists for not making their music unified. Verdi had to make a choice (conscious or unconscious as the case may be), between monothematic structure and melodic spontaneity, as did Bruckner between unity and "naive disjointed grandeur." They could not, in the nature of the case, have both; and ought implies can. In general, the point is that there may perfectly well be mutually exclusive features which are nevertheless *both* good-making; nor is this characteristic of aesthetic contexts alone. Faustian striving and Stoic resignation may both be virtues, although they cannot both be exemplified in the same man.

(3) The third objection that I wish to consider grows out of the following situation. Suppose that a listener finds a certain piece of music lacking in unity: not incoherent, but not unified either. Suppose further that I point out to him that the piece in question is monothematic. And suppose, finally, that our listener (who, by the way, is a devoted music-lover of fine aesthetic sensitivity) still describes the piece as lacking in unity. "Yes: it is monothematic," he insists, "but I just would not want to go so far as to say that it is unified; it just doesn't hang together." If such a statement is possible, can the foregoing analysis of unity be correct?

If I had characterized the present situation as one in which the listener perceived the monothematic structure by examining the score, but could not, even after the examination, hear the thematic – harmonic, rhythmic, or serial – relationships as constituting monothematic structure when he listened to the music, we would have a case of what musicians sometimes call "paper unity," music that can be seen but not heard, "music for the eyes." And such a case would cause us no trouble. For when I say that a piece of music has monothematic structure, I mean monothematic structure that can be heard; and when I say that monothematic structure is being perceived, I mean that it is being heard. So discovering paper unity by examining a score is not a case of musically perceiving monothematic structure (unless the person in question is such an accomplished musician that by reading the score he can "hear" the music "in his mind").

It is not, however, the case of paper unity that I am talking about here, for our listener *hears* the monothematic structure. Nevertheless, he denies that the music is unified. How can we allow for the logical possibility of such a case and yet insist that monothematic structure is a necessary-and-sufficient condition for the ascription of musical unity?

Let me begin to answer this question by quoting a statement of Joseph Margolis with which, it is clear, I am in almost complete disagreement. Professor Margolis writes: "... I think that where the contrast [between 'really is' and 'only looks'] is allowed [in an aesthetic context] – as significantly for *balanced, unified,* and the like – the contrast ceases to be a perceptual one, becomes instead valuational."[16] As we have seen, there would seem to be far more to the distinction between being unified and only appearing unified than Margolis allows. What interests me here, nevertheless, is the suggestion that "unified" can function at times in a predominantly evaluative way. The point I want to make is that although "unified" does indeed function in the way I have tried to indicate, it always carries along with it a positive valuational implication as well, since it is a good-making feature. And at times this evaluative function may become the primary one.

If Mr. A were to say "X is unified because it is monothematic," and Mr. B were to insist "X is monothematic but it is not unified," I think we would have a basically evaluative dispute, Mr. A praising X with the honorific term "unified," Mr. B purposely withholding praise with the more neutral term "monothematic." Later on I shall consider such situations in a more general context, pointing out that they are not by any means exclusively aesthethic in nature and hence need not raise any particular problem for the condition-governed model of aesthetic terms. It must suffice now to be very short with the objection under discussion. Where unity is denied in the acknowledged presence of monothematic structure, what is being denied is simply a certain degree of aesthetic approval.

Monothematic Structure and the Condition-Governed Model

We have until this point been treating monothematic structure as a property the possession of which is a necessary-and-sufficient condition for being unified, much in the same way being an integer greater

---

[16] Joseph Margolis, "Sibley on Aesthetic Perception," *Journal of Aesthetics and Art Criticism,* XXV (1966), p. 158.

than one and having no factors other than itself and one are necessary-and-sufficient conditions for being a prime number. But, clearly, this will not do, for it is at variance with our thesis that terms such as "unified" are *not* condition-governed in this way. Our paradigm case of a condition-governed term is "intelligent"; and there is no single feature, or closed group of features that can be called the necessary-and-sufficient condition, or the necessary-and-sufficient conditions for intelligence. We must now, in conclusion, reconcile what we have said about musical unity with our condition-governed model. And in order to do this we must unpack the notion of monothematic structure a bit.

We have claimed that monothematic structure is the necessary-and-sufficient condition for being unified. We must now ask, What is the necessary-and-sufficient condition (or set of necessary-and-sufficient conditions) for being monothematic? And the answer is: No such necessary-and-sufficient condition (or set of conditions) exists; for "monothematic" is condition-governed in the very same way that "intelligent" is.

Let us call having monothematic structure being *"m."* Then, given enough *m*-making features, we would be logically compelled to call a composition *m*, just as given enough intelligent-making features, we would be logically compelled to call a man intelligent. But we cannot give an exhaustive list of *m*-maikng features, any more than we can give an exhaustive list of intelligent-making ones. For the list is open-ended: new *m*-making features are continually added under the impact of new musical schools and styles.

So, for example, the unifying features of a Mozart theme-and-variations would be certain enduring segments of the theme; whereas (say) the features which make one recognize the first variation of Brahms's *Variations On a Theme by Haydn* (Opus 56) as a variation of that theme – that is, as being of a "unity" with it – would not, I do not think, be perceived as such by a contemporary of Mozart: it would not be recognized as a variation of the theme at all. The *m*-making features that Brahms could work with were not even on Mozart's list; or, rather, Brahms added to the list when he wrote the first variation of Opus 56. (Actually, the Brahms variations can be thought of, so to speak, as variations in reverse: the earlier variations being more remote from the theme than the later ones.) Again, the *m*-making features of a Haydn rondo are far different from those of a twelve-tone piece, and so on. Nor should we think of *m*-making features as necessarily linear – i.e. "themes" – as the phrase "monothematic structure" might misleadingly suggest. For we include on our list of *m*-making features chordal structures, tone-clusters, and even sonorities and tone colors, when they function organizationally to set up patterns of repetition – many of these, of course, having become *m*-making features only in recent times and being unthinkable as such in (say) the eighteenth century. And we cannot, of course, complete the list – that is the logical structure of the condition-governed model with which we are working.

Thus we can really think of the terms "monothematic" and "unified' as descriptively equivalent: those features which count towards monothematic structure count at the same time towards unity; *m*-making features are unity-making features. But there is, as we have seen, this crucial difference between the judgments "Unified" and "Monothematic." The former bestows merit and the latter does not; the former is used to pass a positive verdict, the latter a neutral one. And this of course is why Mr. A and Mr. B can agree about what organizational features X has and yet Mr. A can conclude "Unified" while Mr. B can conclude "Monothematic but not unified."

But suppose we conclude that a composition is not unified (does not possess monothematic structure) and does not even *appear* particularly unified. We might still be loath to say that it is or appears chaotic. There is, of course, nothing particularly disturbing in this, any more than there would be in saying that Mr. C is neither intelligent nor gives the appearance of intelligence, yet nevertheless is not stupid or stupid in appearance.

However, there may be more to it than that. We might contrast, for example, the closely knit, unified structure of Bach's *Goldberg Varia-tions* with the overture and rather amorphous collection of separate movements which constitute Beethoven's *Creatures of Prometheus* ballet music (Opus 43). And I think we would want to say that *Prome-theus* lacks not only the "real" unity of the *Goldberg Variations* but also that very palpable "apparent" unity which Tovey perceived in Verdi's *Stabat Mater*. But now compare *Prometheus* with (say) an eighteenth-century opera pastiche which might consist of contributions from two or more different and even uncontemporaneous composers. We would be likely to say that in some sense or other *Prometheus* is unified and the pastiche is not. Nor is that sense hard to locate. We would want to say that *Prometheus* at least has stylistic unity, being the work of one composer during one discrete period of his creative life, whereas the pastiche has little stylistic unity, how little, of course, depending upon how unlike the styles of the contributors might be.

And there are other musical "unities": the unity of mood that pervades Bach's *Christmas Oratorio*; the dramatic unity of Beethoven's *Leonore* overtures; and so on.

These uses of "unity" must of course be acknowledged to exist; and to this extent "musical unity" has more than one sense. But in any of these related senses there is no reason to believe that it is not condition-governed. Those features which go to make up structural unity may, of course, be different features than those which go to make up unity of mood or style. Yet there *are* style-making features (for example, Brahm's predilection for two-against-three), and mood-making features (notice the overwhelming predominance of the major key in the *Christmas Oratorio*), and beyond a certain point we would not, I suspect, be logically free to deny unity of style or mood. But establishing this would require more musical spade-work; and I wish to go no further along such lines here. What I hoped to do was establish the conditions governing what appears to be the hard-core sense of "unified" as applied to music, and that case I am now content to rest.

Recapitulation

The purpose of the present chapter has been to defend, by example, the thesis that the terms we use to describe works of art are condition-governed. We began by distinguishing three ways in which a term might be said to be governed by conditions: (1) the way in which "prime number" is governed by the logically necessary-and-sufficient conditions "integer greater than one and having no factors other than itself and one"; (2) the way in which "intelligent" is governed by an "open-ended" set of conditions; (3) the way in which "red" and other color words are governed by conditions of normal perception and perceiver. We settled on the second as our model, and we chose unity in music as our test case.

If our analysis is correct thus far, we can consider it as established that the term "unity" as applied in musical contexts is condition-governed. But "unity" belongs to a large class of terms, yet to be clearly delineated, and it is this entire class with which we are concerned, for our thesis is that each member of this class, like "unity," is condition-governed. We cannot, however, hope to examine each and every member in the same detail that we have examined musical unity, even if, *per impossibile*, we could make an exhaustive list of them. What we *can* do is demarcate this class of terms more precisely and determine, at least, that there are no obviously compelling reasons why each member should *not* be subsumed under the condition-governed model. To these two tasks we now turn; they will occupy the remainder of this study.

TWO CONCEPTS OF TASTE

Taste and Non-taste

There are vastly many terms used to describe painting, literature, music, and the like. They might, it has been argued, be divided into two groups: those ("unity" among them) the correct application of which it seems appropriate to represent as requiring "taste," or aesthetic "sensitivity" of some kind, and those whose application seems to require nothing more than the five senses, functioning normally, and a sound mind. Thus Frank Sibley writes, in what bids fair to emerge as one of the most capable and fruitful aesthetic studies of recent years:

We say that a novel has a great number of characters and deals with life in a manufacturing town; that a painting uses pale colors, predominantly blues and greens, and has kneeling figures in the foreground; that the theme in a fugue is inverted at such a point and that there is a stretto at the close; that the action of a play takes place in the span of one day and that there is a reconciliation scene in the fifth act. Such remarks may be made by, and such features pointed out to, anyone with normal eyes, ears, and intelligence. On the other hand, we also say that a poem is tightly-knit or deeply moving; that a picture lacks balance, or has a certain serenity and repose, or that the grouping of the figures sets up an exciting tension; that the characters in a novel never really come to life, or that a certain episode strikes a false note. It would be neutral enough to say that the making of such judgments as these requires the exercise of taste, perceptiveness, or sensitivity, of aesthetic discrimination or appreciation; one would not say this of my first group.[1]

That it might seem appropriate to represent certain terms in our language as (in certain contexts) requiring "taste" or aesthetic "sensitivity" for their application is surely interesting in itself. More interesting still is the claim, for which the distinction between taste

---

[1] Frank Sibley, "Aesthetic Concepts," pp. 63–64. Cf. Sibley, "Aesthetic and Nonaesthetic," *The Philosophical Review*, LXXIV (1965), p. 135.

and non-taste provides the departure point, that these same terms display some rather unusual (if not unique) linguistic behaviour: that they are not condition-governed even in a weak way; that no description in non-taste-terms ever entails a taste-term (although a description in non-taste-terms may entail the negation of a taste-term). It is this general claim that we want to examine closely in the following chapters; for we already have some reason to doubt its validity since at least one taste-term, "unity," has been shown to be governed by conditions. But it is important, before such an examination can be undertaken, or, rather, as the first step in that examination, to determine just what influence the concept of taste exerts on the claim that taste-terms are non-condition-governed.

That some conceptual relationship does indeed hold between taste and the (supposed) non-condition-governed behavior of taste-terms is at least hinted at by Sibley. I say "hinted at" because it never really comes out into the open; but it lurks not too far beneath the surface, as a look at the following passage will indicate.

It is at least noteworthy that in applying words like "lazy" or "intelligent" to new and unique instances we say that we are required to exercise judgment; it would indeed be odd to say that we are exercising *taste*. In exercising judgment we are called upon to weigh pros and cons against each other, and perhaps sometimes to decide whether a quite new feature is to be counted as weighing on one side or the other. But this goes to show that, though we may learn from and rely upon samples and precedents rather than a set of stated conditions, we are not out of the realm of general conditions and guiding principles. ...

Nothing like this is possible with aesthetic terms. Examples undoubtedly play a crucial role in giving us a grasp of these concepts; but we do not and cannot derive from these examples conditions and principles, however complex, which will enable us, if we are consistent, to apply the terms even to some new cases.[2]

It is clear that Sibley sees some kind of conceptual connection between judgment and the presence of conditions governing the applications of such terms as "lazy" or "intelligent," on the one hand, and, on the other, taste and the absence of such conditions. It is inappropriate, Sibley argues, to say that taste is required to tell if someone is lazy or intelligent, but appropriate to say that judgment is required. And in exercising judgment we are "called upon" to do certain things which "show that ... we are not out of the realm of general conditions"; that is, we apply terms governed by conditions. Contrariwise, it *is* appropriate to say that taste is required to tell if something is p or q,

---

[2] "Aesthetic Concepts," p. 72.

where p and q are "aesthetic terms" like "unified." Presumably, if the symmetry of the argument is to be preserved, it would be *inappropriate* to say judgment was required. And here we no longer have conditions to govern the applications of our terms. So it would seem that there is a connection between it being appropriate to ascribe the exercise of judgment (but not taste) to telling whether someone is lazy or intelligent and the fact that "lazy" and "intelligent" are condition-governed; and likewise that there is a connection between it being appropriate to ascribe the exercise of taste (but not judgment) to telling whether something is (say) graceful or delicate and the fact (if indeed it is a fact) that "graceful" and "delicate" are not condition-governed. What can that connection be?

There are some very common phrases containing the term "taste," the most well-known, I suppose, being "There is no disputing about taste." If, one is tempted to argue, the concept of taste with which we are here concerned is the concept encapsulated in the above formula, the connection would be quite obvious. For if Mr. A says "X is p," and Mr. B says "X is not-p," and if being p or not-p is simply "a matter of taste," in the sense of there being no disputing about tastes, this is tantamount to there being no intersubjective conditions governing the application of p. So if one merely exercises one's taste in deciding whether X is p, one appeals to no conditions; and if it is *appropriate* to say that telling whether something is p requires taste, then it would seem to follow that p is non-condition-governed; or, rather, the conditions governing p are simply the likes and dislikes of those using it.

Sibley, however, explicitly states that it is not this concept of taste to which he refers: "When I speak of taste," he writes,

... I shall not be dealing with questions which center upon expressions like "a matter of taste" (meaning, roughly, a matter of personal preference or liking). It is with an ability to *notice* or *see* or *tell* that things have certain qualities that I am concerned.[3]

But if the connection between taste in the first sense, and the non-condition-governed behavior of terms *seems*, at least, fairly clear, the connection between taste in the second sense and such behavior is not by any means so obvious. Nor, it must be added, is it altogether obvious that Sibley believes such a connection in fact exists. All I have been willing to say in this regard is that he "hints at" some kind of

---

[3] *Ibid.*, p. 65.

connection; and I do not want to hang an interpretation of him on anything so tenuous as that. So it would be well as this point to drop, for a while, any pretense of attributing any position to anyone, and simply to raise the question what, if any, connection exists between the concept of taste and the supposed non-condition-governed behavior of taste-terms, independent of whether Sibley or anyone else believes there to be a connection. I will argue that there is no connection: that if taste-terms *are* non-condition-governed, the exercise of taste or aesthetic sensitivity in no way lends support to the claim that they are.

An Ability to Notice or See or Tell

Let us begin with what Sibley calls the "ability to *notice* or *see* or *tell* that things have certain qualities." It is clear that we attribute such abilities in many other contexts besides the context of the fine arts – in many contexts where the term "taste" would be quite odd and out of place. The term "taste" is, of course, very much at home in the world of art, and has been since antiquity. But we speak of taste – good taste, bad taste, exquisite taste, lack of taste, and so on – not only in literature and painting and music: we praise a person's taste in wine, or in women, or in horseflesh; and it is very doubtful that we mean anything "aesthetic" by it. Yet it would indeed be odd to say that our perceiving of someone's laziness or intelligence was due to good taste in people. In this Sibley is certainly correct. However, one wonders: Would it be any less odd to say that being able to tell whether a horse will make a jumper or not is due to good taste in horses? Yet we do say that so-and-so has good taste in horses; taste and horses do mix. The question is: Do we ever attribute the perceiving of *any* "quality" to taste? – any quality save two, that is: the "qualities" of *goodness* and *badness*. If someone *likes* certain horses, we say that he has good taste in horses. If he likes certain women, we say that he has good taste in women. If he likes Bach, some would say that he has good taste in music. Thus we tend to praise someone for his taste in X's if he likes the same X's we like, or if he likes the X's we think are good, or if he thinks the same X's are good we think are good. But someone who thought Whirlaway might make a good jumper or thought Bach's music majestic would neither be praised nor blamed for his *taste*, whether we agreed with him or not. But this is not because the concept of taste is out of place in company with horses or music. People's taste is praised or blamed for their liking or not liking certain things, or for their thinking them good or bad, not for their recognizing properties in them. It is a mistake to think that we ordinarily call *any* ability to *notice* or *see* or *tell* that things have certain qualities by the name of "taste," except the ability to notice or see or tell that things have the qualities of goodness and badness (if qualities they be).

How an aesthetician might fall prey to this error is not hard to imagine. When "taste" first gained wide currency as a critical term, in seventeenth-century France, it was associated with an ability to *evaluate*, which is indeed faithful to its culinary origins. But it became associated too, early on, with the adumbration of an aesthetic value theory – a theory which conceived of aesthetic value terms as naming very subtle features of works of art for which the phrase *je ne sais quoi* was frequently used. In nature and art "these mysterious qualities ... produce the effect of beauty or ugliness, [and so to speak], cause in us mysterious feelings of inclination or aversion which are beyond reason and which the will cannot control," wrote Dominique Bouhours in 1671.[4] "Taste" very soon hardened into a faculty; and although it remained for the most part a faculty of evaluation, evaluation was generally conceived as involving special aesthetic qualities which aesthetic value terms named. Thus there are well-entrenched historical precedents which make it natural for the aesthetician to think of "taste" as the name for an ability to notice or see or tell that aesthetic things have certain *qualities*. How natural, then, to use it as a name for the ability to notice or see or tell that aesthetic things have qualities other than simply the qualities of aesthetic goodness or badness; and so the concept of taste is wrenched from its original place in the realm of evaluation and appreciation and deposited in the realm of aesthetic perception.

There is, of course, nothing wrong with using the term "taste" in this way. The mistake lies in the belief that this is a pre-systematic ordinary language use. And it is a mistake that has clearly done some mischief. For if we say that it sounds odd to attribute the perception of intelligence or laziness to "taste," and then point out that it is not odd to attribute the perception of delicacy in painting, or majesty in music to "taste," we are making a very parochial and, therefore, misleading statement indeed, one that does not, so far as I

4 Dominique Bouhours, *Entretiens d'Ariste et d'Eugènie*, in *The Continental Model*, ed. Scott Elledge and Donald Schier (Minneapolis: University of Minnesota Press, 1960), p. 235.

can see, tap the conceptual reservoir of ordinary linguistic usage. It may not sound odd to the aesthetician to say that taste is required to perceive such qualities as delicacy; but it is, I submit, because the aesthetician has become used to a technical sense of "taste" which ordinary language users do not share. The terms, then, over which the concept of taste ranges are value and preference terms alone, in ordinary language, not terms like "unified" and "delicate." Thus the implications of taste for the behavior of the terms to which it is appropriate in ordinary language are completely irrelevant to us, as we are interested only in the latter.

We have seen that it sounds odd to attribute the perception of any features of an object to taste save those which are entirely evaluative, like goodness and badness, or beauty and ugliness. It is with our evaluations, and with our likes and dislikes, we have argued, that the term "taste" seems to be associated. Nevertheless, we must add, there are certain cases of evaluation in which we would hardly say that "taste" was being exercised. It would be odd, for example, to say that someone had good taste in shovels, or in lawyers; and it would be odd too, I should think, if someone were said to have bad taste in people if he thought Caligula was a good man. Perhaps – though this is merely conjecture – "taste" is an inappropriate concept where evaluations are either wholly utilitarian or wholly moral. It is appropriate, I suppose, where some kind of enjoyment is connected in some intimate way with an evaluation (but not necessarily implying that the enjoyment is the bestower of value). However this looks like it will turn out to be a complicated matter, and pursuing it will take us too far from our topic.

It would be well, therefore, to drop the term "taste," at least for the time being, as a name for any ability to notice or see or tell that things have features like delicacy, garishness, unity and the like. We need not, however, abandon our original question. For there *are* terms which we use to name abilities over and above those of the five normally functioning senses and sound mind – abilities to perceive various features of the world and its inhabitants. We say that so-and-so has "insight" into people or "intuitions" about certain things or fine aesthetic "sensitivity." And we might usefully ask what the applicability of such concepts suggests about the terms we use to describe the features they are applicable to.

However, once the aura of "taste" is removed, there seems little temptation to say that unusual ability in the way of aesthetic perception suggests the terms we use to describe works of art are non-condition-governed, any more than unusual ability in noticing or seeing or telling things about people or dogs suggests the non-condition-governed behavior of the terms we use to describe people and dogs. Mr. A may be able to detect how intelligent or lazy someone is after only the briefest observations; and Mr. B may be able to tell immediately whether a strange dog is vicious or not. Yet no one would want to say that "intelligent," "lazy," or "vicious" are non-condition-governed terms because of this. It is because people turn out to have the features whose presence determines us to affix the terms "intelligent," "lazy," and the like, that Mr. A has gained his reputation for unusual insight into people; and it is because dogs turn out to have the features whose presence determines us to affix terms like "vicious" that Mr. B has earned his reputation for intuitions about animals. When there are features the presence of which compels us to conclude that someone or something is p or q, we say that p and q are condition-governed terms. And to say that someone has a special knack for telling whether someone or something is or is not p or q hardly suggest that p and q are non-condition-governed, where p and q are, for example, "intelligent" and "vicious." Why then should the requiring of the knack we call "aesthetic sensitivity" suggest that aesthetic p's and q's are non-condition-governed?

It might be replied that there certainly is one use of the term "intuition" which does indeed suggest a lack of intersubjective tests: the use to which the term has been put by certain philosophers (and others) to explain the perception of such qualities as moral good and evil, or the awareness of some kind of "reality" inaccessible to the normal perceptual faculties. But this is clearly a technical use of "intuit" (as is Sibley's use of "taste"); and it is with the ordinary use – which suggests no such thing – that I am concerned. As a matter of fact, it is the supposed non-condition-governed behavior of terms which tends to suggest some "special" faculty of intuition, rather than the faculty suggesting the non-condition-governed behavior. We are driven to intuitionism by things which seem to require some kind of desperate measure. Be that as it may, all I am arguing here is that there is nothing about the ordinary use of such concepts as intuition, insight, sensitivity, and the like, that suggests the non-conditon-governed behavior of terms for whose application they are deemed appropriate.

There is one further point, however, that must be cleared up before we can rest content with this conclusion. We should distinguish, I think, between two situations in which it might be appropriate to ascribe some *noticing* or *seeing* or *telling* to a special ability not possessed by every normal man. For this purpose let us contrast Mr. A's insight into people and Mr. B's intuitions about animals with Mr. C's talent for mathematics.

It seems appropriate to ascribe Mr. A's perceiving of intelligence or laziness to an insight into people; and, likewise, it seems appropriate to ascribe Mr. B's perceiving of Beaumont's viciousness to his intuitions. But in saying insight was necessary for doing what Mr. A does, I surely am not suggesting that only those gifted with Mr. A's kind of insight can recognize laziness or intelligence. I would mean, rather, that insight is necessary for doing it in the extraordinarily short time Mr. A requires to make his determinations. Likewise for Mr. B's intuitions about animals. I can always check up on either Mr. A or Mr. B by ascertaining, in my own humdrum way, whether or not the individuals Mr. A calls intelligent or lazy have the features whose presence warrants our calling them intelligent or lazy, and whether or not Beaumont has the features whose presence warrants our calling him vicious. And it is clear from the way I check up on Mr. A and Mr. B that the terms they use to describe people and dogs are condition-governed.

What of Mr. C's talent for mathematics? Of course only those with mathematical ability can verify Mr. C's talent for mathematics, although they do it in much the same way I verify Mr. A's insights and Mr. B's intuitions. The difference is that every normal person can recognize intelligence and laziness in people, and viciousness in dogs; but not every normal human being can perceive the things mathematicians perceive. So to a vast number of perfectly normal people, Mr. C's talent for mathematics can only be accepted on authority. Nevertheless, when non-mathematicians speak of a talent for mathematics, they do not mean that there are no conditions governing mathematicians' uses of terms, though they can never know what these conditions are.

A group of specialists, like mathematicians, of course has its own sub-group of unusually gifted practitioners. What Newton could intuit directly, Halley required a proof to see. But this raises no further problem for us. Halley was merely doing what the normal observer does when he verifies Mr. A's insight or Mr. B's intuitions, although anyone can check up on Mr. A or Mr. B, whereas only a mathematician can check up on Mr. Newton.

Where then does the talent we call aesthetic sensitivity fit into all of this? Is it akin to Mr. A's insight and Mr. B's intuition? Or to Mr. C's talent? It is a nice question; and, fortunately, we need not essay a complete answer here. But it will be useful to pursue it briefly.

If I say "Mr. A has mathematical ability," I am not saying that he can do simple arithmetic, although a person whose only mathematical accomplishment is simple arithmetic can truthfully be said to "have mathematical ability" – *some* mathematical ability. But when I ordinarily take the trouble to say that someone has mathematical ability, I mean to say that he has a talent above the average, out of the ordinary. It is the same, one would think, with the notion of aesthetic sensitivity. If I were to say "Mr. B has aesthetic sensitivity," I would mean that he possesses an unusual ability to make aesthetic distinctions, although all normal people have a modicum of aesthetic sensitivity – some ability to make aesthetic distinctions (like "dumpy" or "graceful"). Thus, when I say "Mr. A has mathematical ability," or "Mr. B has aesthetic sensitivity," I would mean, presumably, that they are distinguished beyond the average abilities of people in those areas. And the same, of course, is *obviously* true of such statements as "Mr. C has insight into people," or "Mr. D has intuitions about animals"; for "insight" and "intuition" are words which signify not just "ability" but extraordinary ability, unusually acute perception.

Now when I say "Mr. A has mathematical ability," I may be suggesting two things: (1) that Mr. A can do or see things the average person can do or see, but do or see them in an unusual way, for example do arithmetic mentally, "see" without paper what the outcome of a sum will be, do a sum or "see" the answer unusually quickly, or without ever making an error; (2) that Mr. A can do things, or see things, that the ordinary person cannot do or see at all, for example, that Mr. A can do tensor analysis, or "see" that the gambler's fallacy really is a fallacy. Ordinarily, I am only suggesting the former when I say "Mr. C has insight into people" or "Mr. D has intuitions about animals." Am I suggesting both when I say "Mr. D has aesthetic sensitivity"? In this respect, is "Mr. B has aesthetic sensitivity" like "Mr. A has mathematical ability" or like "Mr. C has insight into people" and "Mr. D has intuitions about animals"? Certainly I *may* be suggesting the latter, namely, that Mr. B sees things that the average person cannot see (like Bunthorne transfixed before what to us ordinary lumps is a commonplace object with no aesthetic qualities). And it is this kind of seeing that causes perplexity. For if Mr. B simply sees things that we can see, but sees them sooner, we can verify that they are really there by (eventually) seeing them for ourselves. This is not so in the latter case. I say "Mr. A sees p's that non-p-seers cannot see in virtue of a special p-seeing faculty which non-p-seers do not have." Mr. A says "X is p"; and I ask myself "How do *I* know that he is right – that X really is p?" If I say "It must be p, because Mr. A says it is p and Mr. A has the p-seeing faculty," I am in danger of launching myself into the intuitionist's all-too-familiar vicious circle. *I* cannot see p. Mr. A says that he can. *He* has the p-seeing faculty. But how can I verify "X is p" if I cannot see p for myself? Well at least I will get some push in that direction by being shown that Mr. A really has this faculty that I do not have, i.e. the p-seeing faculty – and there's the rub. *If* the only evidence I have that Mr. A has the p-seeing faculty is that he claims to see p, then his evidence for "X is p" is his possession of the p-seeing faculty, and his evidence for having the p-seeing faculty is his claim that X is p.

At times we may all feel ourselves in this same situation when we take the mathematician's, or any other expert's word for it that he sees things we cannot see in virtue of possessing an inborn ability we do not share. But only madmen really think that mathematicians are conspirators or dupes who have bamboozled the world or themselves into believing they see relationships which in fact are not there at all. When the ordinary man, untainted with intuitionism, says "Mr. A has mathematical ability," he is not suggesting with his words that Mr. A applies mathematical terms by an occult faculty; and there is no reason to believe when he says "Mr. B has aesthetic sensitivity" he is suggesting any such thing either.

Of course we *do* have evidence that mathematicians see things we cannot see. But, to be on the safe side, let us not commit ourselves to the view that we have evidence for believing people with unusual aesthetic sensitivity see things we cannot see. For that is not the point; the point is that *merely* because we ascribe aesthetic seeing to a special ability we call aesthetic sensitivity, we are not in a position to say *anything* about the behavior of aesthetic terms. Perhaps aesthetic sensitivity is neither like mathematical ability, on the one hand, nor like insight into people and intuitions about animals on the other. *Perhaps* it is different in that the terms we use to describe people and dogs, and mathematicians use to describe whatever it is they do describe, are condition-governed terms whereas the terms we use to describe works of art are non-condition-governed. That would be an interesting conclusion. But we would be finding out about the talent by way of the terms, not the terms by way of the talent (which is the strategy we are trying to evaluate). All I am arguing here is that whether aesthetic terms are non-condition-governed is a question quite independent of whether it is appropriate to ascribe the perception of features which these terms name to aesthetic sensitivity: a special ability to notice or see or tell that things have certain qualities.

De Gustibus

We have, till now, been discussing an aesthetic ability to notice or see or tell which Sibley called (mistakenly) "taste" – mistakenly, that is, if he was not using a coined word (albeit an old coin) but intending to use "taste" in its ordinary-language sense. We come now to that ordinary sense of "taste," encapsulated in the age-old dictum, *De gustibus non est disputandum*, the sense Sibley explicitly disavowed. It is important, I think, for us to give this concept of taste our careful scrutiny, despite Sibley's disclaimers. For I suspect it of wielding a secret and unwholesome influence on the aesthetic climate; and clearing the air will be a good thing to do. What I will be trying to show in this section is that even the terms over which the ordinary concept of taste *does* range are not, because taste is appropriate to them, non-condition-governed; and, hence, even *if* taste were (which it is not) an ability to notice or see or tell that things have qualities (other than the qualities of goodness and badness), it still would not suggest that the terms which name these qualities are non-condition-governed.

Let me begin with a slight historical detour. I have already alluded to the growth of "taste" as a critical concept in seventeenth-century France. That growth was very rapid: before the end of the seventeenth century full-blown theories abounded; and the wide swath cut by the concept of taste through the Enlightenment is well-known – particularly well-known to philosophers through Hume's masterful essay "Of the Standard of Taste" (1757).

Hume recognized that preference and aversion play some part in the evaluations we make of art works. But he recognized too that to define "good work of art" and "bad work of art" merely in terms of *any* man's preferences and aversions flies in the face of common sense and linguistic usage.

According to the dispositions of the organs, the same object may be both sweet and bitter; and the proverb has justly determined it to be fruitless to dispute concerning tastes. It is very natural, and even quite necessary, to extend this axiom to mental, as well as bodily taste; and thus common sense, which is so often at variance with philosophy, especially with the sceptical kind, is found, in one instance at least, to agree in pronouncing the same decision.

But though this axiom, by passing into a proverb, seems to have attained the sanction of common sense; there is certainly a species of common sense, which opposes it, at least serves to modify and restrain it. Whoever would assert an equality of genius and elegance between Ogilby and Milton, or Bunyan and Addison, would be thought to defend no less an extravagance than if he had maintained a mole-hill to be as high as Teneriffe, or a pond as extensive as the ocean. ... The Principle of the natural equality of tastes is then totally forgot, and while we admit it on some occasions, where the objects seem near an equality, it appears an extravagant paradox, or rather a palpable absurdity, where objects so disproportionate are compared together.[5]

Hume in particular, and the eighteenth century in general, had an insight into the *De gustibus* formula which prevented them from mistaking the force of the *non est disputandum*. It is particularly true of Hume that he recognized the appropriateness of saying, at times, "There is no disputing about tastes," with reference to works of art, but recognized too its inappropriateness at other times. Nor did Hume merely redefine "taste" to suit his own philosophical purposes. Rather, he had a genuine insight, as the above passage reveals, into common sense – ordinary linguistic – usage, and took his philosophical cue from that.

Consider now the following conversational snippets:

(1) Mr. A. This artichoke is delicious.
     Mr. B. No, it isn't nice at all.
     Mr. A. Well, there is no disputing about tastes.
(2) Mr. A. Shakespeare was the greatest poet who ever lived.
     Mr. B. Edgar Guest was the greatest poet who ever lived.
     Mr. A. Well, there is no disputing about tastes.
(3) Mr. A. Bach is the greatest composer who ever lived.
     Mr. B. Beethoven is the greatest composer who ever lived.
     Mr. A. Well, there is no disputing about tastes.

Now only in (1) does it sound entirely right to say "Well, there is no disputing about tastes." But discussions about the goodness or badness of artichokes, and poets, and composers are *all* discussions where *De gustibus* ... or some variation of it might be appropriate; and there is nothing odd in saying someone has good taste in foods, literature, or music. So it is not the subject matter that determines the appropriate-

---

[5] David Hume, "Of the Standard of Taste," *Of the Standard of Taste, and Other Essays*, ed. John W. Lenz (New York: Bobbs -Merrill,1965), pp. 6–7. For a more detailed analysis of Hume's argument, here, see Peter Kivy, "Hume's Standard of Taste: Breaking the Circle," *The British Journal of Aesthetics*, VII (1967).

ness or inappropriateness here. Rather, what is crucial seems to be the point at which such remarks are introduced, the appropriate point being the point at which reasons have been exhausted. It is entirely appropriate in (1) because Mr. A is making a personal-preference remark, pure and simple. Cases (2) and (3) however are another story. These are the kind that exercised Hume. To assert that there is no disputing about tastes "where objects so disproportionate are compared together," as in case (2), for instance, is, Hume claims, "a palpable absurdity." But "where the objects seem near an equality," as in case (3), there is no absurdity at all in appealing, for a decision, to "the natural equality of tastes," that is, to admit dispute, reasoned argument, is not possible. For here the reasons on one side can be expected to balance the reasons on the other; and hence to fall on one side of the argument or the other can only be the result of inclination, preference or aversion, in other words, merely a matter of taste. Where two critics, equally qualified and informed, disagree in such a situation, as Mr. A and Mr. B, we have reached the end of reason's tether. As Hume puts it, "where there is such a diversity in the internal frame or external situation as is entirely blameless on both sides, and leaves no room to give one the preference above the other; in that case a certain degree of diversity in judgment is unavoidable, and we seek in vain for a standard, by which we can reconcile the contrary sentiments."[6]

Hume is, I think, barking up the right tree; but it will be instructive to get a closer look at the quarry. Why is it inappropriate, "a palpable absurdity," to say "Well, there is no disputing about tastes" when Mr. A claims that Shakespeare is the greatest poet and Mr. B that Edgar Guest is? Because, clearly, it suggests that there are no reasons to be given for Mr. A's assertion, and this is simply not the case. Rhythm, imagery, psychological insight - the whole critic's arsenal has yet to be mobilized by Mr. A. And the same, really, is true of case (3). Of course there are reasons to support the judgment that Bach is the greatest of all composers, and reasons to support the candidacy of Beethoven too. It is inappropriate in case (3) to say "Well, there is no disputing about tastes" *if* case (3) represents the *beginning* of an argument. Hume's "equality of objects" is indicated when the reasons on one side counterbalance those on the other: an outcome that we do not envision in case (2) but do in case (3) – which is why *De gustibus* ... does not strike quite the discordant note in the latter that it does in the former.

[6] Hume, *op. cit.*, pp. 19–20.

Nor, by the way, are such considerations limited to artists and artichokes. Was Don Budge a greater tennis player than Pancho Gonzales? Well, it's all a matter of taste, isn't it? It's a toss up, in other words. But that does not suggest there are no reasons for saying Don Budge was great, or Pancho Gonzales was. It does not suggest that "great tennis player" is a non-condition-governed concept, or that the terms we use to describe the features of tennis players are non-condition-governed. "There is no disputing about tastes" is not so much a phrase that demands a particular subject matter as one that demands a particular context. It is not appropriate for artichokes but inappropriate for tennis players. It is appropriate for indicating in disputes about both of these (and other things as well) the point at which reasons have been exhausted. It is appropriate for indicating that there are no further reasons to give, not that there are no reasons to give at all. In short, the concept of taste encapsulated in such phrases as "There is no disputing about tastes" does not imply or suggest that the terms over which it ranges are non-condition-governed; rather, that they are condition-governed up to a point. Thus even if "taste" were the appropriate name for an ability to notice or see or tell that things have such qualities as unity, it would not in the least suggest that "unity" and the like are non-condition-governed terms.

Recapitulation

It has been argued by Sibley and others that there is a distinctive appropriateness in the ascription of taste or aesthetic sensitivity to the perception of certain features, but not to the perception of certain others. Further, and more important, it has been argued that those terms the application of which it seems appropriate to describe as requiring taste or aesthetic sensitivity are characterized too by being non-condition-governed. And although not explicitly held by Sibley, it might be held that there is some conceptual connection between a term's requiring for its application taste or aesthetic sensitivity and its being non-condition-governed (if indeed it is non-condition-governed).

Our conclusion in this chapter has been that the appropriateness of ascribing taste or aesthetic sensitivity to the application of some range of terms or other in no way suggests that the terms are non-condition-governed. If indeed they are, other arguments will be required to establish that they are. Of such arguments there is no dearth; and to some of them we now turn our attention.

CHAPTER III

ARE AESTHETIC TERMS UNGOVERNABLE?

Aesthetic and Nonaesthetic

In the preceding chapter I discussed a distinction between terms the correct application of which it seemed appropriate to ascribe to some special aesthetic sensitivity and terms the application of which seemed to require only the normal five bodily senses and a normally endowed mental capacity. I called the former "taste-terms," and the latter "non-taste-terms," and I shall continue to do so, though it must be borne in mind that in so doing I will be using a coined word. I shall mean by a taste-term a term the correct application of which requires a special ability to, as Sibley puts it, notice or see or tell that things have certain qualities. And, as I have tried to show, "taste" does not ordinarily mean that at all. But no harm will be done so long as my use of "taste" is not confused with the ordinary use; so long as no conclusions are drawn which are said to follow from the concept (or concepts) of taste embodied in ordinary language.

With this minor point out of the way, we now come to a major one: the relationship of *taste* and *non-taste* to *aesthetic* and *nonaesthetic*. It is in fact just to keep from begging a very important question that I have so far chosen to call the terms whose application seems to require special perceptual abilities "taste-terms" and refrained as much as possible from calling them "aesthetic terms" (as Sibley does). For one might very well want to maintain that the two are not co-extensive: that in a perfectly reasonable and philosophically interesting sense of "aesthetic" and "nonaesthetic," not all taste-terms are aesthetic terms and not all non-taste-terms nonaesthetic terms. I do not wish to foreclose on this possibility.

I shall be interested only in the terms we use to describe works of art. Of course, the art-world does not have a separate language from the rest of us; and most words used to describe works of art are used to describe other things as well. One can say that a barn is red and a painting is red; that the country is unified and the *Eroica* is unified; that Michelangelo's David *weighs* two tons and Lindbergh's *Spirit of St. Louis* weighs two tons; that Millet's *The Gleaners* is "'natural and convincing"[1] and that the President of the United States at his press conference was natural and convincing; and so on. By a "taste-term" I shall mean *any* term used to describe a work of art the application of which it seems appropriate to ascribe to an ability over and above the five senses and normal mental capacities. By a "non-taste-term" I shall mean any term used to describe a work of art the application of which seems to require no such ability. An example of the former might be "unified," an example of the latter "red."

Now Sibley claims that all taste-terms are non-condition-governed; and he elects to call *all* such terms "aesthetic terms." His terminology would be completely uncontroversial if "aesthetic" did not drag along with it so many philosophical problems. But the fact is that philosophers have been trying since the eighteenth century to make some kind of important distinction between the aesthetic and the nonaesthetic. So by coupling "aesthetic" with "non-condition-governed," one immediately suggests that a solution to a long-standing problem is being proffered. Nor is that solution out of touch with the tradition. For something quite important seems to follow from the contention that aesthetic terms are non-condition-governed, namely, that it makes no sense to distinguish between being p and only seeming p, where p is an aesthetic term – a claim that we have already met in the particular case of musical unity. We can only conclude that X really isn't p, although it seems p, by seeing that the conditions for being p are not present; and likewise we can only conclude that X really is p and doesn't merely seem p by seeing that the conditions for being p are present. And if p is non-condition-governed, we would not be logically able to do this. In this implication, the claim that aesthetic terms are non-condition-governed dovetails with one of the most frequently recurring approaches to the distinction between aesthetic and non-aesthetic, an approach that has its beginnings in the eighteenth century and is already fully developed in Kant's *Critique of Judgment*. I refer to the claim that in aesthetic contemplation or perception, we are interested only in the "appearances" of things and that, therefore, from the aesthetic point of view, to appear p is to be p, and vice versa. I shall have

---

[1] E. H. Gombrich, *The Story of Art* (London: the Phaidon Press, 1952), p. 383.

occasion to discuss this again, at some length, in a subsequent chapter. It is only necessary here to recognize the relation between baptizing taste-terms "aesthetic," and the traditional attempt to distinguish the aesthetic from the nonaesthetic.

In order to avoid the suggestion that the distinction between taste and non-taste necessarily demarcates also the line between aesthetic and nonaesthetic, it would be well to eschew the phrases "aesthetic term" and "nonaesthetic term" altogether. But this would needlessly obfuscate the discussion of Sibley's position and the positions of many who have been influenced by him and his terminology. I shall therefore accept the equation of "taste-term" with "aesthetic term," and "non-taste-term" with "nonaesthetic term," under the assumption that "aesthetic" and "nonaesthetic" are being used in a sense completely neutral as regards the traditional attempt to spell out the notions of aesthetic experience, aesthetic contemplation, aesthetic perception, and the like.

In the present chapter I will be examining Professor Sibley's arguments, based for the most part on linguistic usage, that aesthetic terms are not condition-governed. I shall be claiming that his arguments are inconclusive. As a prelude, I want now to make two preliminary claims: (1) that at least one term which Sibley conceives of as a non-taste-term, and hence condition-governed, is in fact a taste-term *and* clearly condition-governed; and (2) that at least one term which Sibley conceives of as a taste-term is not a taste-term in any very obvious sense, and nevertheless seems clearly to be an aesthetic term. Establishing these preliminary claims will serve a double purpose. It will immediately cast doubt on any argument purporting to show that *all* taste-terms are non-condition-governed; and will support our suspicions concerning the identification of taste-terms with aesthetic terms (in any non-trivial sense of "aesthetic").

(1) In a passage quoted previously, Sibley enumerates some of the remarks we make about works of art which, according to him, are made without the aid of taste or aesthetic sensitivity. We say of a fugue, for example, "that there is a stretto at the close. ..." The term "stretto," when applied to a fugue, is defined in the *Harvard Dictionary of Music* as "the imitation of the subject in close succession, with the answer coming in before the subject is completed."[2] That "stretto"

---

[2] Willi Apel, *The Harvard Dictionary of Music* (Cambridge, Mass.: Harvard University Press, 1951), p. 711.

is a condition-governed term seems clear enough from this admirably terse formula, although we must not be misled by the apparent tightness of the dictionary definition into thinking that there are logically necessary-and-sufficient conditions. For when the subject of a fugue is "completed" – i.e. what exact succession of notes constitutes the subject of a fugue – is vague enough to make "stretto" condition-governed only in our second way, not in the way in which "prime number" (say) is governed by logically clinching conditions. But condition-governed it is; and it does not, therefore, qualify as a taste-term (or aesthetic term) according to Sibley: so a stretto can be "pointed out to" and perceived by "anyone with normal eyes, ears, and intelligence." No special ability to notice or see or tell that things have certain qualities is required, on Sibley's view, to hear strettos.

This is patently false: to hear strettos and other details of musical structure requires more than practice; it requires a musical "ear." There are people with the perceptual faculties of deer stalkers and diamond cutters, with minds like steel traps, and who are not tone-deaf; and some of these people, I submit, could not hear when the stretto comes any more than they could read your mind. It appears to me incontestable that the term "stretto" is a condition-governed term the correct application of which it seems entirely appropriate to ascribe to taste or aesthetic sensibility, a special ability to notice or see or tell that things have certain qualities. In face of Mr. B's continued inability to hear strettos (and other such musical features) in spite of patient instruction, it seems altogether correct linguistic usage for Mr. A to finally conclude: "Mr. B simply does not have an ear for music – he lacks musical sensitivity." Thus "stretto" is a taste-term, but condition-governed too.

It might, of course, be possible to teach even a deaf person to tell (but not hear) whether a fugue has a stretto by giving him a mechanical technique for recognizing when the black marks on a printed page of music indicate a stretto. He would not be able to hear a stretto but could tell whether or not a fugue contained one, much in the same way that a blind person might tell by scientific instruments (in Braille) whether or not something is red, although, of course, he can never see that it is red. And what we can teach a deaf person to do we can certainly teach a tone-deaf person, as well as a person who lacks musical sensitivity: lacks a musical ear. None of them could hear if a fugue had a stretto or not, although they could tell it by examining the score and applying some rule of thumb. Thus my argument merely shows that one cannot *hear* a stretto without a special ability we call an "ear" for music and which is the musical counterpart of aesthetic sensitivity. It does not show that one cannot discover in other ways that a fugue has a stretto. However, when we say that someone has a special ability to notice or see or tell that music has certain qualities, surely what we mean to assert is that he has an ability to *hear* those qualities. Our conclusion, then, is that at least one musical taste-term is condition-governed.

(2) The term "graceful" Sibley considers an aesthetic term; it is, there-fore, on his view, non-condition-governed and, of course, a taste-term. Let us grant for the moment that it is non-condition-governed. Are Sibley (and others) correct in maintaining that taste or aesthetic sensitivity is required for its application. Well, who has ever met a "normal" person, man or boy, who has not been able to use the word correctly? If that is not evidence that no special ability is required for its application, I do not know what "special ability" means. To be sure, a handicapper may not recognize grace in a minuet; but he can recognize it in a three-year-old. It would be a mistake – a mistake which, I hasten to add, Sibley does not make – to assume that aesthetic distinctions are all unusual or esoteric. Sibley himself writes:

We learn while quite young to use many aesthetic words. ... They are not rarities; some ranges of them are in regular use in everyday discourse.[3]

"Graceful" is just such a word, and its widespread use *suggests* at least that no special talent is required to use it correctly. Nor, it might be argued, would we say that an adult who could not use the word cor-rectly was lacking in taste or aesthetic sensitivity, in any special ability to notice or see or tell that things have certain qualities. We would say, rather, that he had extremely poor eyesight, or was not very bright, or did not know English. Thus we have in the term "graceful" – and there are, I am sure, many terms very much like it in this respect – a term which we would want to call "aesthetic" in some perfectly reasonable (but, I confess, wholly intuitive) sense, and yet which we would not want to say requires any special aesthetic sensitivity for its application.

We have, with these preliminary claims, been so far only snapping at Sibley's heels. In order to bring him down we shall have to do more than merely pick out a term here or there about which he is mistaken

---

[3] "Aesthetic Concepts," p. 78.

in one way or another. Nor, of course, can we hope to examine every term individually and refute Sibley by enumeration. We must critically examine the arguments whereby Sibley and others have tried to establish the non-condition-governed behavior of aesthetic terms. If we can show that these arguments do not establish any such thing, we can conclude that whether or not these terms are non-condition-governed is at least an open question. To that task we must now turn.

Aesthetic Terms and Aesthetic Discourse

In this and the following two sections I want to state as carefully as I can Sibley's thesis (now rather widely accepted) that aesthetic terms are non-condition-governed, state the arguments (also widely accepted) which he gives in support of it, and, finally, state my own reasons for dissenting from Sibley's view. The arguments examined and (ultimately) rejected are those contained in section I of Sibley's much commented upon article "Aesthetic Concepts." I have separated these arguments into three kinds: (1) those involving the general nature of aesthetic discourse; (2) those involving the question of how we apply aesthetic terms to novel objects; and (3) those involving the relationship of aesthetic terms to taste and appreciation.

Before I approach these topics, however, I want to say something about Sibley's method, and the method of my reply. What Sibley does in the section of "Aesthetic Concepts" with which I am presently concerned is, essentially, to exhibit some linguistic facts about aesthetic discourse and explain these facts on the hypothesis that aesthetic terms are not condition-governed. What I will argue is that interpreted in certain ways Sibley's putative facts are indeed facts of linguistic behavior, but that we need not claim aesthetic terms are non-condition-governed in order to account for them. And interpreted in other ways, I shall argue, they are not facts of linguistic behavior at all. My conclusion, then, will be that at least in the ways I have interpreted Sibley's linguistic facts, they in no way suggest the non-condition-governed behavior of aesthetic terms.

Sibley begins by distinguishing, as we have already done, between two kinds of condition-governed terms: those (like "equilateral triangle" or "prime number") for the correct application of which there are logically necessary-and-sufficient conditions; and those (like "intelligent") for the correct application of which there are no necessary-

and-sufficient conditions "but for which there are a number of relevant features, A, B, C, D, E, such that the presence of some groups or combinations of these features is sufficient for the application of the concept."[4] We are already familiar with the salient characteristics of these two condition-governed models, so there is no need for us now to examine them further. And later on Sibley introduces another group of condition-governed concepts which we have not felt it necessary to discuss at all, called by H.L.A. Hart "defeasible," in that "A, B, and C together are sufficient for the concept to apply *unless* some feature is present which overrides or voids them."[5] The time is long past, I think, when anyone would insist that aesthetic terms must apply in virtue of one or even a set of logically clinching conditions obtaining. Sibley dismisses peremtorily the possibility that aesthetic terms are condition-governed in this way;[6] and in choosing to defend a looser condition-governed model, I have tacitly acquiesced in this. Nor do I want to contest Sibley's denial that aesthetic terms are defeasible.[7] For defeasible concepts are associated intimately with the legal and moral language of responsibility and excuses – which seems very remote indeed from art-talk. Only the second possibility has remained a real option (if aesthetic terms are condition-governed at all). That is why I have plumped for it and why Sibley concerns himself almost exclusively with it in his denial that aesthetic terms are condition-governed.

Our paradigm case of a condition-governed term – and Sibley's paradigm as well – is the term "intelligent." For such a term, as we have seen, we cannot name any one feature which would be sufficient and/or necessary; nor can we enumerate any discrete group of features and say: "Here is the complete set of features necessary-and-sufficient." But, again, because the list of features which count towards being intelligent is an open one, forever incomplete, it does not follow that we are never in a position to conclude with something like logical certainty that someone is intelligent. Each intelligent-making feature, though never by itself necessary or sufficient, always represents a small step in the direction of intelligence; and when these small steps carry us beyond a certain point we are in a position where we cannot deny the appropriate predicate.

---

[4] *Ibid.*, pp. 66–67.
[5] *Ibid.*, pp. 70–71.
[6] *Ibid.*, p. 66.
[7] *Ibid.*, pp. 70–71.

With regard to aesthetic terms, however, the situation is quite different, according to Sibley. "There are," he writes,

no sufficient conditions, no non-aesthetic features such that the presence of some set or numbers of them will beyond question logically justify or warrant the application of an aesthetic term. . . . Things may be described to us in non-aesthetic terms as fully as we please but we are not thereby put in the position of having to admit (or being unable to deny) that they are delicate or graceful or garish or exquisitely balanced.[8]

There *is* a way in which aesthetic terms *are* condition-governed; but it is a negative rather than a positive way. That is to say, although no description in nonaesthetic terms ever implies an aesthetic description, it might imply the negation of an aesthetic description:

For instance, it may be impossible that a thing should be garish if all its colors are pale pastels, or flamboyant if all its lines are straight. There may be, that is, descriptions using only non-aesthetic terms which are incompatible with descriptions employing certain aesthetic terms.[9]

And there are features which count only towards, never against a given aesthetic term, much in the way that being able to do mathematics can only count for, never against intelligence. But, Sibley concludes, "Although there is this sense in which slimness, lightness, lack of intensity of color, and so on, count towards, not against delicacy, these features, I shall say, at best count only *typically* or *characteristically* towards delicacy; they do not count towards it in the same sense as condition-features count towards laziness or intelligence; that is, no group of them is ever logically sufficient."[10]

So far Sibley has simply laid it down as fact that aesthetic terms are non-condition-governed; there has been no real appeal to argument of any kind. He is now ready to present, if not an argument, at least an elucidation of his position. This is in the form of what can best be represented as two hypothetical cases.

Case (1):

an object which is described very fully, but exclusively in terms of qualities characteristic of delicacy, may turn out on inspection to be not delicate at all, but anemic or insipid.[11]

Sibley's contention in case (1) can be summarized along somewhat the following lines: Terms like "intelligent" are condition-governed in that

[8] *Ibid.*, pp. 67–68.
[9] *Ibid.*, p. 68.
[10] *Ibid.*, p. 69.
[11] *Ibid.*

given the presence of enough features counting towards intelligence, the ascription of the term cannot be withheld; but "delicate," "unified," and the like, are non-condition-governed in that there never are enough (nonaesthetic) features counting towards them to compel their ascription; for one can always apply instead some other term towards which these features also count. That this is true of the term "delicate" (for example) is left to the linguistic intuition of the reader. It is a linguistic fact, presumably, which any user of the language will recognize on reflection. Whether this is really the case we shall have occasion later to discuss.

(Case 2):

A painting which has only the kind of features one would associate with vigor and energy but which even so fails to be vigorous and energetic *need* not have some other character, need not be instead, say, strident or chaotic. It may fail to have any particular character whatever.[12]

Now a painting *and* a person may of course fail to have any of the characteristics toward which their features count simply because not enough of these features are present. A person might have only those features which count towards being brooding or melancholy, and yet not have enough of them to make him either brooding or melancholy. Likewise, a painting might have only features which count towards being vigorous and energetic and strident, and yet not have enough of them to make it vigorous or energetic or strident. There is nothing exceptionable in this. There is nothing in either of these two examples to make us say that the terms in question are non-condition-governed (nor would Sibley want to claim this with regard to terms like "brooding" and "melancholy").

I will take case (2), then, to be an illustration of the claim that an object of aesthetic predication, no matter how many nonaesthetic features it might have counting towards aesthetic features p, q, and r, might remain characterless, whereas such a situation could not occur with condition-governed terms like "lazy" or "intelligent." Beyond a certain point, that is, we could not continue to claim that a person was characterless, whereas we might with regard to an object of aesthetic predication. Again, this (supposed) linguistic fact is not argued for but left to be perceived by the language-user.

It appears to me that taken in one way case (1) is certainly an accurate characterization of aesthetic discourse. But what it establishes on this

12 *Ibid.*, p. 70.

interpretation is not that terms like "delicate" and "unified" behave differently from terms like "intelligent" and "lazy"; rather, that they behave exactly alike. What I am arguing, then, is that these considerations of Sibley's establish, really, the parity of these terms: that if "intelligent" or "lazy" is a paradigm case of a condition-governed term, then "delicate" or "unified" must be condition-governed in the very same sense; and that if we are going to insist on calling "delicate" and "unified" non-condition-governed, we are going to be compelled to call "intelligent" and "lazy" non-condition-governed as well, in which case this sense of "condition-governed" will dissolve, and we will be saying very little in saying that aesthetic terms are non-condition-governed, least of all that they are any different in this respect from nonaesthetic terms.

Suppose that Mr. A ticks off a long list of Mr. B's features - features which A claims are a clear indication of Mr. B's laziness. But Mr. C, although he concurs in bestowing all of these features on B, nevertheless concludes that B is not lazy at all. There would be nothing odd in this; to deny that Mr. B is lazy is not necessarily to assert that he is energetic or dynamic. C might, for example, grant that B is "phlegmatic" but deny that he is "lazy" – and he might name the very same features of B in support of his claim as A names in support of his. Likewise, Mr. A might claim (to use Sibley's example) that an object is "delicate" whereas Mr. C insists that it is "anemic," while both name the same nonaesthetic features in support of their judgments. What would make this case an odd one would be for Mr. C to claim (say) that the object is "ponderous" or "clumsy." To deny that an object is delicate is not to assert that it is the opposite of delicate, any more than to deny that someone is lazy is to assert that he is the opposite of lazy.

There is a very familiar way of describing such situations. We might say A and C do not disagree about how to *describe* B – that is, they do not disagree as to what features B possesses – but only disagree in attitude towards B, A having an attitude of disapproval and bestowing the negative term "lazy" on him, C having an attitude of approval or at least of neutrality and bestowing the positive or neutral term "phlegmatic" instead. Likewise, we might say A and C do not disagree as to what features belong to the object which A wants to call "delicate" and C "anemic"; but A expresses a positive attitude towards it by using the honorific term "delicate," and C expresses disapprobation with the negative "anemic." And *if* by a term being non-condition-governed we mean that such a situation can arise, then "lazy" is no less non-condition-governed than is "delicate." If not, then there seems to be no good reason to conclude from case (1) that "delicate" is non-condition-governed; for that is all Sibley's example seems to involve.

The above representation of the situation might perhaps be rejected because it is based upon what has become a very fuzzy and suspect distinction, namely, that between evaluative and descriptive uses of language; or because the distinction between disagreement in beliefs and disagreement in attitudes is likewise vague and difficult to pin down. And I have no wish to argue these points; for there is no need to represent the situation in just this way. But however we do decide to describe it, sauce for the goose must be sauce for the gander: the fact will remain that "lazy" and many other perfectly ordinary terms like it behave in the same way as "delicate" does in case (1). A certain indeterminacy is in evidence. If this behavior is taken as a sign that "delicate" is non-condition-governed, then it should be taken as a sign that "lazy" is non-condition-governed as well; if, on the other hand, we insist that "lazy" is a paradigm case of a condition-governed term, then this behavior cannot very well be taken as a sign that a term is non-condition-governed since "lazy" exhibits such behavior too.

Let me now turn for a moment to case (2) before pursuing case (1) further. As I mentioned when it was first introduced, it seems oddly unconvincing if taken in its most obvious sense. *Of course* a painting might have only those features counting towards some aesthetic quality or other and be characterless nevertheless, just as a person might have only those features counting towards some quality and be characterless nevertheless. On this interpretation case (2) clearly indicates that aesthetic terms are on the same logical footing as, for example, condition-governed terms naming personal attributes like laziness, intelligence, and so forth. For this reason, at the risk of setting up a straw man, I have interpreted case (2) as exemplifying the claim that it is logically possible for an aesthetic object to be characterless no matter how many features it may possess counting towards some given aesthetic predicate, although nothing of this kind could obtain in regard to condition-governed terms like "lazy" or "intelligent."

Why should we accept this claim? Do aesthetic terms really behave in this quite extraordinary way? Surely the logic of aesthetic terms allows that an aesthetic object may be characterless even though it possesses features counting towards some aesthetic quality (and only possesses those features). But surely it is the same logic that allows for a similar case to arise anent a person. And it is the logic of "Close but no cigar," not the logic of "No cigar no matter what." Perhaps five features counting towards "lazy" or "phlegmatic" are not enough, and ten are. Perhaps ten features counting towards vigor or stridency are not enough and fifteen are. But are there really *never* enough? Recall the case of the *Eroica's* unity. The main theme of the first movement, as Grove points out, recurs "no less than thirty-seven times." Are we still logically free to deny that it is unified and declare it characterless. If *any* movement of that length were to have its main subject recur thirty-seven times, would we still be logically free to deny that it is unified and declare it characterless? I suggest that the answer is an emphatic "No."

Thus case (2) can be dismissed as impotent in establishing the non-condition-governed behavior of aesthetic terms (if indeed it was so intended). Case (1), however, may still have some mileage left in it; so I will revert to it now, and pursue it a bit further.

We have seen that being condition-governed does not preclude the possibility of two (or more) *related* terms being applied correctly to the same object whether the terms are aesthetic or nonaesthetic. Thus Mr. A would be logically free to call Mr. B "lazy," and Mr. C logically free to call him "phlegmatic," although both terms are condition-governed and each is entailed by the same description of Mr. B. What Mr. A and Mr. C would *not* be logically free to do would be to call Mr. B (say) "energetic" or "lively." These latter terms are ruled out: Mr. B's features are incompatible with them; but they are compatible both with "lazy" and with "phlegmatic" which, on that account, are called *related* terms. And the same can be said of related aesthetic terms like "delicate" and "anemic," or "vivid" and "garish," the first of each pair expressing a positive attitude, the second a negative one, although the same features which could be cited to support the one could be cited to support the other. I suggested that disagreements as to whether Mr. B is "lazy" or "phlegmatic," whether an object is "delicate" or "anemic," "vivid" or "garish," be seen as disagreements in attitude or evaluation. However that may be, the aesthetic and nonaesthetic terms are on a par in this regard, and we must seek elsewhere for a reason to call the latter condition-governed and the former not.

One such reason might be supposed to lie in the relation of aesthetic perception to aesthetic judgment. To find out if a painting is delicate you must, one would think, look at the painting, not read a description of it. Thus Sibley: "Though on *seeing* the picture we might say, and rightly, that it is delicate or serene or restful or sickly or insipid, no *description* in non-aesthetic terms permits us to claim that these or any other aesthetic terms must undeniably apply to it."[13] One feels, somehow, that it does a kind of basic logical injustice to the notion of aesthetic judgment to claim that a mere description, sans direct inspection, can entail anything really consequential about a work of art.

Yet we can hold that a description implies "X is p" (where p is an aesthetic term) without at the same time denying that we cannot ever be certain, prior to direct inspection, of X really being p. For what we are saying about X when we say that such-and-such a description implies "X is p" is that *if* X answers the description, then p will be applicable to X. But whether or not X answers to the description is something, of course, that can only be determined by direct inspection.

The very same point, obviously, can be made with regard to non-aesthetic terms like "lazy" and "intelligent," indicating once again that there is no very palpable difference in logical behavior. No matter how thorough a description of Mr. B is given, would not the possibility always remain open of Mr. A's opinion that he (B) is lazy changing when A meets B and observes him at first hand? Certainly if when A observes B he indeed turns out to have all of the features he was represented to A as having, then A is not free to deny "B is p" where p is "lazy" *or some related term* (e.g. "phlegmatic"). For, by hypothesis, *that* description compelled A to call him p; that is what we mean when we say p is a condition-governed term. But if what A's observation of B reveals is that he (B) lacks some of the p-making features he was represented as having, then of course it is possible for A to revise his judgment that B is p. So when we say that direct inspection of B might always justify A's withdrawing a predicate indicated by a description, we can only mean that the description can always turn out to be a misdescription in some crucial respect.

What, then, are we to say of the analogous aesthetic term? Clearly, we must hold that it is *always* subject to withdrawal on direct inspection, even when the description is in no need of revision, if we are to contrast it with the former case and hold that the aesthetic term is non-condition governed. Is that really tenable? There can be no doubt that "delicate," like "lazy," is always subject to withdrawal when direct inspection reveals a misdescription. But this does not show that non-aesthetic descriptions never imply aesthetic descriptions – merely that

[13] *Ibid.*, p. 68.

nonaesthetic descriptions are not always accurate. And it seems incredible that inspection of the aesthetic object, even if it reveals no novel nonaesthetic features whatever, even if it disappoints none of our description-based expectations of nonaesthetic features, nevertheless holds out the possibility of our withdrawing the indicated aesthetic term (or terms). Again: Are we really logically free to deny that the first movement of the *Eroica* is unified, if, on inspection, Grove's description turns out to be accurate and the first movement does indeed contain "no less than thirty-seven" recurrences of the main theme? To answer "yes" would, it seems to me, misrepresent critical discourse and the aesthetic discourse of the plain man.

Now the nub of my argument is that the representation of aesthetic terms as being completely free of governing conditions stretches credulity to the breaking point: we just don't talk that way about art. To this it might be replied that the situation is not quite so desperate as I have painted it. For it is Sibley's contention that no description in nonaesthetic (non-taste-) terms ever logically compels us to apply an an aesthetic (taste-) term, although a description which contains some *aesthetic* terms might. So, this argument would go, there *are* cases in which one might conclude from a description that a work of art is p (where p is an aesthetic term): cases in which the description contained at least one aesthetic term. Thus, although direct inspection of a work of art which disappointed none of our description-based expectations of nonaesthetic qualities would still permit us to withhold an aesthetic term (and its related terms), one which disappointed none of our expectations of aesthetic qualities would not. In short, the argument is that aesthetic terms *are* condition-governed, but the conditions are aesthetic rather than nonaesthetic.

The problem with this, I think, is that if a term is condition-governed there must be intersubjective criteria for determining whether or not the term properly applies in a given instance. And to show that descriptions containing aesthetic terms imply other descriptions implying other aesthetic terms fails to show that aesthetic terms are condition-governed because it fails to reveal any intersubjective criteria whatever. Suppose I say "X is p," where p is an aesthetic predicate. Suppose I support this claim by saying "X is q and r, and being q and r entails being p," where q and r are also aesthetic terms. How am I to verify that X is q and r? If q and r are aesthetic terms, and if no description in nonaesthetic terms ever entails an aesthetic term, then either I must appeal to *other* aesthetic terms that entail q and r, which begins to look like an infinite regress; or I must simply appeal to my taste or aesthetic sensitivity as some kind of infallible intuitive faculty. In neither case have I appealed to any intersubjective criteria. For by hypothesis the only intersubjective criteria are to be found in the application of non-aesthetic terms which require for their application only the natural mental and physical faculties whose objective status is vouchsafed by the conditions of normal perception and perceiver. Thus, although aesthetic descriptions may be implied by other aesthetic descriptions, aesthetic terms remain non-condition-governed unless they are governed by nonaesthetic terms. To be governed by aesthetic terms alone, if aesthetic terms are construed as Sibley construes them, is not to be governed by conditions that can be verified intersubjectively: hence is not to be governed by conditions, really, at all.

One further point here. Doubtless, only very slight changes in an object's nonaesthetic qualities will justify our withdrawing one aesthetic term and replacing it with another, whereas such a slight alteration (say) as Mr. B's not really being able to read French after all is not of itself likely to force a revision in our estimate of his intelligence. In art, as Sibley observes, "even a slight change might make all the difference."[14] However, this is a contingent fact about art, not a fact about the logical behavior of aesthetic terms. One might just as well argue that the terms we use to describe people's personalities are non-condition-governed because only very slight changes in people's behavior is likely to cause revisions in our estimates of their personalities. The behavior of "lazy" or "intelligent" may be more stable than that of "delicate" – but it is of no conceptual significance.

Aesthetic Terms and Novel Objects

We come now to what Sibley considers a crucial question for his analysis: How do we apply terms to novel cases? I know that Jones and Smith are intelligent. How can I tell whether to apply the term to the new boy? And what of "delicate," "unified," and other aesthetic terms? How do I come to apply *them* to new cases? The question is a crucial one for this reason. If the application of terms to new cases turns out to be a significantly different matter for terms like "intelligent" and "lazy" than for terms like "delicate," "unified," and the like, and if we can explain this difference only on the assumption that

[14] *Ibid.*, p. 75.

"lazy" and "intelligent" are condition-governed, and "delicate" and "unified" are not, then Sibley has won his point.

Sibley maintains, to start with, that there is a prima facie similarity between terms like "intelligent" and aesthetic terms in their application to new cases. Neither kind of term can be applied to new cases in a rigid, mechanical way, as for example, "prime number" can:

> to exhibit a mastery of one of these concepts we must be able to go ahead and apply the word correctly to new individual cases, at least to central ones; and each new case may be a uniquely different object just as each intelligent child or student may differ from others in relevant features and exhibit a unique combination of kinds and degrees of achievement and ability. In dealing with these new cases mechanical rules and procedures would be useless; we have to exercise our judgment guided by a complex set of examples and precedents. Here there is a *superficial* similarity to aesthetic concepts. For in using aesthetic terms too we learn from samples and examples, not rules, and we have to apply them, likewise, without guidance by rules or readily applicable procedures to new and unique instances.[15]

Just what the precise procedure is whereby we apply the term "intelligent" (say) to new cases Sibley does not tell us in any great detail. Later on we will attempt to remedy this somewhat by giving it a firmer outline, for the purpose of showing that it contains nothing that is incompatible with the behavior of aesthetic terms. But we should have his general characterization before us now so that we can see why Sibley believes aesthetic terms cannot be accommodated by it. He writes:

> though we may learn from and rely upon samples and precedents rather than a set of stated conditions, we are not out of the realm of general conditions and guiding principles. ... To profit by precedents we have to understand them; and we must argue consistently from case to case. ... Thus it is possible, even with these very loosely condition-governed concepts, to take clear or paradigm cases of X and say "this is X because ...," and follow it up with an account of features which logically clinch the matter.[16]

So in spite of a surface resemblance between such terms as "intelligent" and aesthetic terms when applied to new cases, we can see again emerging the familiar claim of Sibley's that even "loosely" condition-governed terms can be in some sense "logically clinched," whereas aesthetic terms cannot.

> Examples undoubtedly play a crucial role in giving us a grasp of these [aesthetic] concepts; but we do not and cannot derive from these examples conditions and principles, however complex, which will enable us, if we are con-

---

[15] *Ibid.*, pp. 71–72.
[16] *Ibid.*, p. 72.

sistent, to apply the terms even to some new cases. When, with a clear case of something which is in fact graceful or balanced or tightly-knit, someone tells me why it is, what features make it so, it is always possible for me to wonder whether in spite of these features, it really is graceful, balanced, and so on. No such features logically clinch the matter.[17]

And again: it is apparently left to the language-user to see that aesthetic terms in fact behave in this way and terms like "intelligent" and "lazy" do not. The point is not argued but, presumably, will be apparent to anyone who knows the meaning of "intelligent," "grace-ful," and the like.

Before we attempt to evaluate Sibley's claim that condition-governed terms like "lazy" and "intelligent" are applied to new cases in a signi-ficantly different manner from terms like "delicate" and "unified," it is important to distinguish at least roughly between various kinds of new cases, for, among other things, a brave new world may be new to thee but not to me. When Paris heard the *Rite of Spring* in 1913, it was new to everyone; when Mozart heard Bach's *Singet dem Herrn* in Leipzig it was new to him but familiar to Leipzig.

It would be well to observe too that Sibley emphasizes, to the point, really, of overemphasis, the "uniquely" new. But surely it is true neither of personal first-hearings or seeings or readings, nor of world pre-mieres that the new object is always "strange," "novel," "unique," or anything else of the kind. Although there may be some mild surprises, there is not likely to be much shock value in listening to a Mozart sym-phony for the first time if you are at all familiar with the Haydn-Mozart style or just musically acculturated in a minimal degree. And although the *Rite of Spring* sent its first-night audience out howling with indigna-tion, it is extremely doubtful that a first-performance of Bach or Sibelius ever had any such effect. Some new aesthetic encounters are indeed shocking and startlingly new; however one falls prey to a phony Romantic mystique in believing that this is the rule rather than the ex-ception, even with regard to great works of art.

Among both personal first-hearings and world premieres, then, we will find two kinds of new cases, shading one into the other by degree: there are those which, though new in the sense of never before ex-perienced, are nevertheless in some familiar idiom or style; and those which are new in the sense of novel or unique – relatively unintegrated with the perceiver's previous experience. With regard to the former it

---

[17] *Ibid.*

seems fairly clear that what goes on when we apply aesthetic terms to new cases can be represented without any trouble by a condition-governed model. And although such terms as "novel" and "unique" raise a good deal of dust, I do not believe the latter kind of new case will be recalcitrant either. But let us take the easier kind first.

Consider, for example, a musically sophisticated listener's first encounter with Mozart's G minor Symphony (K. 550). If he does a little homework before the concert he may find that according to one critic it has "a dark and restless quality."[18] Suppose now that our listener gives his first hearing to the work with this description in mind, and confirms for himself that it is indeed "dark and restless." I suggest that what he has done is made use of his previous experience of dark and restless works – his samples and precedents, if you like – from which, albeit vaguely and unconsciously, he has distilled conditions for the applications of these terms. He finds, in listening to the new work, that it fulfills enough of these conditions to be described as dark and restless. Does this representation do any injustice to the musical experience? Sibley gives us no evidence to show that it does. And I ask the reader, if he is also a listener, to see if it does any injustice to his experience of music. It does no injustice to mine.

But let me guard here against a misinterpretation. I am not offering a description of what "runs through the listener's mind"; if I were I doubt I would say anything like what I have just said (although I have no clear idea what exactly I would say). What I am saying is this: that we can represent the logic (not the psychology) of the listener's application of aesthetic terms to new (but not novel or unique) cases as involving (a) the culling of conditions for their application from works already heard; (b) the determining of whether the conditions for applying an aesthetic term to the new case are fulfilled; (c) on the basis of (b) either withholding or applying the aesthetic term in question. Nor of course is this intended to apply to musical works alone, but to all other works of art as well.

Now what of the unique cases – the cases of novelty so often associated with the premieres of important new works? To me it seems passing strange that such cases should be thought to raise a special problem; for the condition-governed model that we have in mind here was introduced into discussions of art, at least in part, with just such cases in view; and, ironically, it was considered not the least of its virtues that such cases could be handled by it quite smartly. I am think-

[18] Eric Blom, *Mozart* (London: J. M. Dent, 1952), p. 204.

ing here, particularly, of Morris Weitz' important article "The role
of Theory in Aesthetics." Weitz' subject is not "aesthetic terms" in our
sense but aesthetic category terms like "novel," "tragedy," and the
term "art" itself. Nevertheless, what he says of these terms, with
regard to unique cases, applies, so far as I can see, *pari passu*, to such
terms as Sibley calls "aesthetic." Weitz writes:

> Consider questions like "Is Dos Passos' *U.S.A.* a novel?," "Is V. Woolf's *To the
> Lighthouse* a novel?," "Is Joyce's *Finnegan's Wake* a novel?" ... what is at stake
> is no factual analysis concerning necessary and sufficient properties but a de-
> cision as to whether the work under examination is similar in certain respects to
> other works, already called "novels," and consequently warrants the extension
> of the concept to cover the new case. ... It is like recognized novels, A, B, C ...,
> in some respects but not like them in others. But then neither were B and C like
> A in some respects when it was decided to extend the concept applied to A to B
> and C. Because work N + 1 (the brand new work) is like A, B, C ... N in certain
> respects – has strands of similarity to them – the concept is extended and a new
> phase of the novel engendered. "Is N + 1 a novel?," then, is no factual, but
> rather a decision problem, where the verdict turns on whether or not we enlarge
> our set of conditions for applying the concept.[19]

It would be well at this juncture to rehearse what we have meant by
"condition-governed," so we can see that Weitz is working here with
the very same notion. A term is condition-governed, on our model, in
that (a) if *enough* features of a certain kind are present in a certain
object we cannot logically withhold the term, although (b) no complete
list of relevant features can be made, the list being an open-ended one.
The term "novel," Weitz is claiming, is just such a term; and its
open-endedness is due, in part, to the fact that new works of art continually contribute new features to the list of features which count
towards being a novel, just as new skills and discoveries contribute new
features to the list of features which count towards being intelligent.
For this reason, two questions might arise in deciding if a new work is
to be counted as a novel or not: (a) Are there enough novel-making
features present to warrant calling the new work a novel? (b) Should
certain features of the new work be added to the list of novel-making
features? The questions are obviously intertwined: in answering "No"
to question (a) we would probably (as a consequence) be answering
"No" to question (b); and in answering "Yes" to question (b) we
would probably (as a consequence) be answering "Yes" to question
(a). But the two questions are, nevertheless, of different logical kinds,
somewhat analogous to J. O. Urmson's distinction between "standard

    [19] Morris Weitz, "The Role of Theory in Aesthetics," reprinted in *Philosophy Looks at
the Arts*, p. 54.

setting" and "standard using":[20] that is, between determining what criteria are going to be relevant to deciding whether or not X is p, and deciding, by means of established criteria, whether or not X is p.

What I want to suggest is that we can treat aesthetic terms, when applied to new "unique" objects, in much the same way Weitz treats category terms like "novel" and "tragedy." The conditions governing aesthetic terms, like those which govern aesthetic category terms, change under the impact of new works. So the questions we are faced with when we wish to describe in aesthetic terms some startlingly new work are the same as those which face us in determining (say) whether *Finnegan's Wake* is a novel or *Death of a Salesman* a tragedy: (a) Are there enough p-making features present to warrant describing the new work as p? (b) Should certain features of the new work be added to the list of p-making features? Thus we cannot, simply by mastering a set of pre-established p-making features, master the use of p; for to say that we have mastered the use of p is to say that we are able to apply p to new cases. And the mastery of pre-established p-making features will not assure that we can. But it does not follow that because mastery of pre-established conditions cannot give complete mastery of a term, the term is not condition-governed. Mastery of a condition-governed term cannot be gained simply by mastering a list of pre-established conditions for its application, because the list is open-ended; and this goes for ordinary terms like "intelligent" and "lazy," aesthetic category terms like "novel" and "tragedy," as well as aesthetic terms like "unified." It is the problem of new cases that brings this out. For mastery of a condition-governed term involves not only "standard using," but "standard setting": not only determining whether there are enough p-making features present to warrant calling something p, but determining whether new features should be added to the p-making list. One of the happy implications of our condition-governed model is that mastery of pre-established conditions cannot guarantee mastery of the term to which they are relevant. This is why the condition-governed model, properly understood, is perfectly adequate in accounting for our ability to apply aesthetic terms to new cases, even where the new cases are of the "unique" and "novel" kind.

---

[20] J. O. Urmson, *The Emotive Theory of Ethics* (New York: Oxford University Press, 1969), pp. 64-67. Urmson is concerned with questions of evaluation, of course, and I am not.

Aesthetic Terms and Taste

Further support for the claim that aesthetic terms are non-condition-governed is given by Sibley in what I shall call case (3). In considering it we will have to reintroduce the topic of "taste" and its relation to the terms to which it is appropriate.

Case (3):

[a] A man who failed to realize the nature of aesthetic concepts ,or someone who, knowing he lacked sensitivity in aesthetic matters, did not want to reveal this lack might by assiduous application and shrewd observations provide himself with some rules and generalizations; and by inductive procedures and intelligent guessing, he might frequently say the right things. But he could have no great confidence or certainty; a slight change in an object might at any time unpredictably ruin his calculations, and he might as easily have been wrong as right. ... [b] He would, for himself, have no more reason to choose tasteful objects, pictures, and so on, than a deaf man would to avoid noisy places. [c] He could not be praised for exercising taste. ... [d] In "appraising" pictures, statuettes, poems, he would be doing something quite different from what other people do when they exercise taste.[21]

I have, for convenience, divided this rather convoluted passage into four separate but related segments; and I shall conclude this account of Sibley's position by glossing them.

(a) A man who lacked aesthetic sensitivity – lacked taste – might master certain rules for the application of aesthetic terms, but although he could thereby "frequently say the right things," he would just as frequently be wrong. Therefore aesthetic terms cannot be rule- (that is, condition-) governed. Taste, not rule-mastery, is the requirement for applying aesthetic terms correctly.

(b) A man who lacked taste and applied aesthetic terms by rules would "have no reason to choose tasteful objects, pictures, and so on." What conclusion we are supposed to draw from this is difficult to make out. Perhaps the following: A man who is applying taste-terms in the "normal" way *would* have reason to choose tasteful objects. A man who is applying taste-terms by rules or conditions has no reason to choose tasteful objects. Therefore, a man who is applying taste-terms by rules or conditions is not applying them in the "normal" way, suggesting that they are not, properly speaking, condition-governed.

(c) A man who lacked taste and applied aesthetic terms by rules and conditions, even when he made the right judgments, "could not be praised for exercising taste." But "normally" a person is praised for his taste when he applies aesthetic terms correctly. Therefore, when a

[21] "Aesthetic Concepts," pp. 72–73.

man applies an aesthetic term correctly on the basis of rules or conditions he is not using that term in the "normal" way, suggesting that aesthetic terms are not rule- or condition-governed.

(d) A man who lacked taste and applied aesthetic terms by rules and conditions, in "appraising" works of art, "would be doing something quite different from what other people do when they exercise taste." Hence he would be doing something "odd"; applying aesthetic terms in this way appears again not to be the "normal" way they are applied; and since this "abnormal" way of applying them is by rules or conditions, it does not appear that aesthetic terms are really rule- or condition-governed, at least not "normally" so.

Now the difficulty here is, clearly, with the notion of taste; and it arises, in part, through the failure to keep distinct the two concepts of taste outlined in the previous chapter.

Let us, for present purposes, abbreviate the kind of taste which Sibley calls an ability to notice or see or tell that things have certian qualities (i.e. aesthetic qualities) $taste_1$, and the kind encapsulated in the phrase *De gustibus non est disputandum* (i.e. a faculty of aesthetic appreciation or value judgment) $taste_2$. And we shall say, further, that the ability to apply aesthetic terms correctly is the necessary-and sufficient condition for having $taste_1$.

Part (a) is, to begin with, a manifest begging of the question *if* the "sensitivity in aesthetic matters" referred to is $taste_1$. For it assumes that we cannot master aesthetic terms by mastering rules and generalizations; that is, it assumes that aesthetic terms are non-condition-governed. But that is just the point at issue. And we have argued that there is no reason to believe mastering rules and generalizations cannot result in mastering aesthetic terms, if we include under that head standard setting as well as standard using. $Taste_1$, we said, is the ability to apply aesthetic terms correctly. And to the extent that one can apply them correctly, one has $taste_1$.

But there is more to part (a) than this; there is, too, I suspect, a confusion of $taste_1$ with $taste_2$. Part (a) only becomes intelligible when this confusion is brought to light.

What could it mean for someone to "know he lacked sensitivity in aesthetic matters" and yet have mastered the rules for the application of aesthetic terms? If our argument is correct, and if "sensitivity in aesthetic matters" is taken to mean $taste_1$, the claim is contradictory. No one can master the rules and generalizations governing aesthetic concepts and fail "to realize the nature of aesthetic concepts," for the one amounts to the other; and no one can master the rules and generalizations governing aesthetic concepts while "knowing he lacked sensitivity in aesthetic matters," for to master the rules and generalizations *is* to have sensitivity in aesthetic matters, that is, taste$_1$.

But suppose that "sensitivity in aesthetic matters" has reference, at least in part, to taste$_2$. Then part (a) becomes *partially* acceptable. For someone might, indeed, realize that "he lacked sensitivity in aesthetic matters," that is, lacked taste$_2$, and yet still master the rules and generalizations governing aesthetic concepts. He would not, however, fail "to realize the nature of aesthetic concepts" if he had, indeed, truly mastered the governing conditions. It seems possible, then, to possess taste$_1$ and lack taste$_2$ – to be able to describe works of art in aesthetic terms and not be able to appreciate or evaluate them. There is nothing logically odd about this, although it might be a rare occurrence.

Following this line of argument, part (b) is seen to be either patently false or trivially true, depending upon how the term "taste" is construed. A person without taste$_2$ would, of course, have no interest at all in works of art even though he possessed taste$_1$ – that is, he would have no appreciation of art. But if he had taste$_2$ he would, of course, have preferences and aversions, regardless of how or whether he could apply aesthetic terms correctly; and hence he would have "reasons" to choose some works of art and reject others. Would a person without taste$_2$ be doing something "odd" in describing works of art? Perhaps; but the oddness would in no way devolve on the manner in which he was applying aesthetic terms – rather in the fact that he was bothering to apply them at all (for, I suppose, the basic motive for describing works of art is an appreciation of, interest in them). And if no oddness is connected with the manner in which aesthetic terms are being applied, we have no reason to think that anything in this manner of applying them – that is, by rules and conditions – is in any way a misrepresentation.

Again, if by "taste" is meant taste$_1$, part (c) seems patently false; for a person *would* be "praised" for his taste to the extent that he indeed could apply aesthetic terms correctly. And a person can apply aesthetic terms correctly on the basis of rules and conditions, if we include under rules and conditions standard setting as well as standard using. Nothing here suggests that applying aesthetic terms by rules or conditions is in any way "odd"; and hence we need not suspect that aesthetic terms, in their normal habitat, are anything but condition-governed.

If, on the other hand, we take "taste" to mean taste$_2$, part (c) becomes trivially true: a person would not be praised for exercising "taste" in applying aesthetic terms correctly, any more than a person who applied color terms correctly would be praised for his musical ear. In short, a person who was exercising taste$_1$ would not be praised for exercising taste$_2$. Now if there is something odd about a person describing works of art even though he has no appreciation of them one way or the other, then a person who is applying aesthetic terms but lacks taste$_2$ is indeed doing something odd. However, as in part (b), the oddness has nothing to do with the fact that he is applying the terms according to rules and conditions; and hence we need not, on account of this oddness, doubt that aesthetic terms are condition-governed.

Part (d) raises, to begin with, a small problem of terminology. We are told that someone "appraising pictures, statuettes, poems," but lacking "taste," would be doing something quite different from someone who appraised such things and was exercising taste in doing so. The notion of *appraisal* immediately suggests *evaluation* – and this adds some confirmation to our thesis that case (3) has not merely been concerned with taste$_1$ but taste$_2$ as well. Yet Sibley has stated quite explicitly that he is not concerned with "verdicts on the merits of works of art. ..."[22] And if we take this disavowal at face value (and there seems no reason not to), we must conclude that by "appraising" works of art Sibley simply means deciding whether or not certain aesthetic terms apply to them, not whether they are good or bad.

In what sense would someone "appraising" works of art sans taste be "doing something quite different" from someone with taste "appraising" them? Again, the answer to such a question requires our deciding how to construe "taste." If taste$_1$ is meant, and if a person is appraising works of art in a reasonably accurate manner, then he simply cannot be appraising works of art sans taste: it is an impossibility. A person who is appraising works of art in a reasonably accurate manner is ipso facto exercising taste$_1$: he is doing the same thing that a man of taste does for he *is* a man of taste. If he is not appraising correctly then he is ipso facto not a man of taste: he is not doing the same thing a man of taste does when he appraises works of art. Is the concept of taste$_1$ somehow incompatible with appraising on the basis of pre-established rules or conditions? I have argued that the notion of a special ability such as taste$_1$ in no way suggests that the terms one applies in exer-

---

[22] *Ibid.*, p. 68. This is reiterated in a subsequent reply to critics, "Aesthetic Concepts: A Rejoinder," *The Philosophical Review*, LXXII (1963), pp. 79–80.

cising it are not condition-governed. If that argument is good, I see no reason to conclude that the man appraising on the basis of pre-established rules or conditions is not exercising taste$_1$. Applying aesthetic terms on the basis of pre-established conditions is not doing something "foreign" to aesthetic sensitivity: it is exercising aesthetic sensitivity.

If, however, the man appraising works of art on the basis of rules and conditions lacks taste$_2$, then part (d) makes a good deal of sense. The tasteless man would be doing something quite different from the man of taste: he would not be *enjoying* (or, for that matter, disliking) works of art – appraising but not appreciating. It is possible to apply aesthetic terms correctly without either liking or disliking works of art, or knowing good works of art from bad. Be that as it may, this is completely irrelevant to the question of whether aesthetic terms are condition-governed. And we need dwell on it no longer.

Recapitulation

Our purpose, in this chapter, was to present in detail some of Frank Sibley's arguments in support of the view that all aesthetic terms are non-condition-governed, and to answer them if we could. We distinguished three basic arguments tending towards the conclusion that aesthetic terms are non-condition-governed:

(1) It is a linguistic fact that no matter how many delicacy-making features (for example) are acknowledged to be present in a work of art, we would always be logically free to call it (say) "anemic" or "insipid" instead.

(2) To be said to understand an aesthetic term, we must be able to apply it to new and novel objects; and this cannot be accommodated by the condition-governed model.

(3) Applying aesthetic terms by following condition-governed rules is incompatible with applying them in the exercise of taste; and since aesthetic terms are taste-terms, they cannot at the same time be condition-governed terms.

In completing our defense of the condition-governed model against these objections of Sibley's, we have in effect completed the heart-piece of our study. But many ancillary arguments remain to be met before we can consider our thesis in any way secure. And to the first of these we next turn our attention.

CHAPTER IV

ARE THINGS ALWAYS WHAT THEY SEEM?

Further Reflections on the Behavior of Aesthetic Terms

Age cannot wither nor custom stale the topic of appearance and reality. It was suggested in the chapter preceding that we would have to open this Pandora's Box. The time has now arrived. Happily we need only open the lid a crack to accommodate our condition-governed model of aesthetic terms. Prudence counsels no more – but necessity demands no less.

The topic of appearance and reality arose for us, it will be recalled, in the following way. If aesthetic terms are not condition-governed, then there is no sense in which we can say "X seems p, although it really isn't," where p is an aesthetic term. For the conclusion "only seems" suggests that there *are* conditions under which we would be compelled to conclude "really is," and that in the case of p these conditions do not obtain. But if p is not condition-governed, there are no conditions to obtain, and the distinction between seeming p and really being p breaks down. On the other hand, if p is condition-governed, even if as a matter of contingent fact no X ever fails to be p, and no perceiver is ever mistaken about an X's being p, it is nevertheless logically possible that an X should fail to be p, and logically possible that an X which fails to be p should appear to some perceiver to be p. If, therefore, one wants to maintain that aesthetic terms are condition-governed, one must also defend the view that the distinction between being p and merely appearing p is a viable one where p is any aesthetic term.

We are primarily concerned with refuting arguments that purport to show aesthetic terms are non-condition-governed. And there are two, a specific and a general one, which might be constructed around the seems-is distinction. The specific argument would be: "Aesthetic terms are not amenable to the seems-is distinction. If aesthetic terms were condition-governed, they would be amenable to that distinction. Therefore, aesthetic terms cannot be condition-governed." The general argument might go something like this: "In aesthetic perception we are only concerned with the way things appear; so in an aesthetic context the distinction between being and appearing is always irrelevant. But if aesthetic terms were condition-governed, the distinction between being and appearing would sometimes be relevant; so it would not be the case that this distinction would always be irrelevant in an aesthetic context. Therefore, aesthetic terms cannot be condition-governed."

In this section of the present chapter I intend to examine the specific argument. In the second and third sections I shall examine the general argument. Concerning both my strategy will the be same: to deny that the distinction between being and appearing is out of place or irrelevant.

In casting about for arguments that attempt to establish the irrelevance of the seems-is distinction for aesthetic terms, we cannot do better than the ones advanced by Isabel Hungerland for thoroughness and insight. It is these that will occupy us here. We adopt for convenience of exposition her abbreviations: "N" (for nonaesthetic term); "A" (for aesthetic term); "N-ascription" (for "X is p," where p is a nonaesthetic term); "A-ascription" (for "X is p," where p is an aesthetic term).

Mrs. Hungerland makes a sharp distinction between aesthetic and nonaesthetic terms closely paralleling Sibley's. She recognizes three prima facie marks of this distinction.[1]

(1) Aesthetic terms usually if not always figure in evaluations; nonaesthetic terms do not.

(2) Aesthetic terms seem to require for their application a special sensitivity or training; nonaesthetic terms do not.

(3) The presence or absence of features named by aesthetic terms does not seem to be determinable by intersubjective tests; this is not the case with features named by nonaesthetic terms.

It is the third of these marks with which we will be concerned.

It is often difficult to make out whether Mrs. Hungerland intends to show aesthetic terms are not intersubjectively determined by showing that they are unamenable to the seems-is distinction, or whether she intends to show they are unamenable to the seems-is distinction by showing

---

[1] "The Logic of Aesthetic Concepts," p. 45.

that they are not determined intersubjectively. I suspect that some-times she is doing the former, sometimes the latter; and as the notion of intersubjective criteria is so intimately bound up with that of the seems-is distinction, there are times when they are quite indistinguish-able – two sides of the same coin. But it is with the attempt to establish that aesthetic terms are not amenable to the seems-is distinction that I am here solely concerned. It is the first premise of what I have called the *specific* argument, the conclusion of which is that aesthetic terms are non-condition-governed. To avoid this conclusion, which is our aim, we must defeat this premise, since the only other premise of the argument, namely, that if aesthetic terms are condition-governed, they would be amenable to the seems-is distinction, appears to me to be unassailable.

The main point of Mrs. Hungerland's with which we are concerned is that "contrasts between *being* and *looking* N have no exact analogue for the A's, that the extension of these contrasts to the field of A's is a metaphoric one only, that the extension is germane not to a common world but to coteries, to shared sensitivities, trainings, and tastes."[2] The key word here, as I shall argue later, is "metaphoric." It is per-fectly clear that we often do make aesthetic remarks – A-ascriptions – of the form "X seems p but really it isn't." Such remarks do not sound odd; there is nothing obviously wrong with them. Mrs. Hungerland is perfectly well aware of this, which is why she cannot insist that the seems-is distinction is *completely* inappropriate to A-ascriptions – rather that it sometimes is appropriate, but only in a "metaphoric" sense.

But "metaphoric" use of the distinction between being and appear-ing is, of course, parasitic on the literal hard-core use (whatever that may be). And it is in explicating the supposed literal use that, I think, Mrs. Hungerland makes a fundamental error. This error has its origin in what begins as an innocent enough restriction on the universe of discourse. Mrs. Hungerland writes, "... I shall, in general, confine my consideration of the A's to those of visual design and of the N's to co-lors...."[3] Now N's, by hypothesis, are amenable to the being-appearing distinction; and in choosing *colors* as her paradigm case of N's, Mrs. Hungerland chooses *being a certain color* and *only appearing a certain color* as her paradigm of the being-appearing distinction. However, because that distinction does not operate in respect to color terms as it

[2] *Ibid.*, p. 50.
[3] *Ibid.*, p. 45.

does in respect to aesthetic terms – and indeed it does not – we need not be driven to the conclusion that it does not apply to aesthetic terms at all, or that it applies in some bogus or "metaphoric" way. There is a good deal with which one can agree in Mrs. Hungerland's very perceptive contrasting of color terms and aesthetic terms. However, the conclusion that the distinction (say) between being red and only appearing red somehow represents *the* standard use against which aesthetic use is to be measured and found wanting seems to me completely unfounded. Before this point is argued, though, Mrs. Hungerland's position must be examined in somewhat more detail.

What is it about color terms that makes them amenable to the being-appearing distinction? It is the fact, already alluded to in the first chapter, that we can state what we take to be the *normal observer* and the *normal perceptual conditions* for color perception. In Mrs. Hungerland's words, "The contrast that will serve to mark off 'N''s like 'red' from 'A''s, is the contrast between looking a certain color to normal observers under normal circumstances (the criteria for asserting that something *is* that color) and merely looking a certain color under special circumstances, say, a blue light, or looking a certain color to non-normal observers, say, the color-blind, under normal circumstances."[4] For "no such general possibility of specifying normal observers and normal circumstances exists for A's, and ... therefore the contrast in question between *merely looking* N and *really being* N has no exact analogue for the A's." Although "there is a good metaphoric extension of the contrast to A's."[5]

In what sense, then, is the extension of the being-appearing distinction to aesthetic terms "metaphoric" only? Let us take some of Mrs. Hungerland's examples: "She only looks elegant to you, she really isn't, because you aren't familiar with haute couture"; "She only looks elegant now, because she's surrounded by all those dowdy women." Why are these not bona fide cases of "only seeming, not really being"? Mrs. Hungerland answers:

the examples call our attention, not to the presence or absence of physical defects in sense organs, but to the presence or absence of common sympathies, snobberies, outlooks, personal history, training in certain arts. Similarly, the norm of circumstances, when we are concerned with A's, cannot be stated in terms of physical viewpoint, lighting arrangements, and so on, but in terms of what we concentrate on, what we disregard, our movement of attention, what might be called our whole "mental stance."

4 *Ibid.*, p. 51.
5 *Ibid.*, p. 52.

Thus: "There are no tests or checks, no logical support for the presence of A's, *literally* analogous to criteria for N-ascribings."[6]

Another way of putting the distinction between N's and A's is to think of N's as establishing our public, stable world, and of A's as being somehow subject-dependent. For this reason

we can for changes in the way things look N to us, decide, or tell a) whether the change is attributable to a change in us or in the object and b) if the change is in us, what sort of change it is, (drugs, odd glasses, abnormal physiology, or just a stand-point different from the privileged or "normal" one for determing *the* – stable or momentary – N in question.) Now when A's change for us (without change of N's) we may be inclined to say that the A-featured "object" has changed, but at the same time, we attribute the change to our own sensibilities.[7]

We seem to be on the verge here of an out and out subjectivism which Mrs. Hungerland is as anxious to reject as I am. Early in her essay she states unequivocally that

the subjective tradition remains unacceptable. The A's are features of perceived objects, of our "outer," not "inner" world.[8]

How can we reconcile the "outerness" of aesthetic features with the fact that we attribute changes in aesthetic objects to changes in "our own sensibilities"? At this juncture Mrs. Hungerland, like many recent writers including Sibley, throws herself into the comforting arms of the Gestalt.

A's belong to the large and heterogeneous family of features studied by gestalt psychologists. This family includes expressive qualities, like the *cheerfulness* of certain combinations of reds and yellows; certain aspects of visual objects that require certain experiences to apprehend, the duck-like look, for example, that a circle and a juxtaposed triangle can have for those familiar with ducks; and features of organization like the tensions between horizontals and verticals in a design, or the movement of a spiral figure, or the figure-and-ground relation of a line on a plane surface, or the recessive effect of patterns on plane surfaces, and so on.[9]

This line of thought is interesting and has given rise to some important developments in recent aesthetic theory (though I do not think it is the panacea it is sometimes made out to be). The following chapter will be devoted entirely to it. Here we need only acknowledge its presence in Mrs. Hungerland's argument and go on to the general conclusion predicated upon it.

[6] *Ibid.*, pp. 52–53.
[7] *Ibid.*, pp. 58–59.
[8] *Ibid.*, p. 54.
[9] *Ibid.*, p. 60.

We have seen that Mrs. Hungerland recognizes the linquistic pro-
priety of the seems-is distinction in regard to aesthetic terms. But, she
maintains, it is a "metaphoric" use only. Nevertheless, if we compare,
for example, "I seem to have a headache" with "The painting seems
garish," we will see that although "seems" is linguistically appropriate
in both, it is not functioning exactly the same way in both. For it is
difficult to imagine a context in which a person could seem *to himself*
to have a headache and really not have one. To say "I seem to have a
headache" as a personal feeling report is the same as to say "I have a
headache."[10] If there is a case in which the seems-is distinction approaches the vanishing point, it is surely here. This vanishing point
has clearly not been approached in our uses of aesthetic terms. What,
then, distinguishes the metaphorical use of the seems-is distinction for
A's, from its literal use for N's, and its degenerate use for personal
feeling reports? Mrs. Hungerland's position is that two requirements
must be fulfilled in the "metaphoric extension of N- to A-ascriptions":
"(a) that the N's which are pre-conditions for the A's in question be
ascribable, truly, to the object described, and (b) that there be stability and community (within an era, a cultural group, a coterie) in
the apprehension of the A's in question."[11] So, for example, if I report
that a painting is "garish" because of colors p, q, and r, and then
find that the painting is not p-, q-, or r-colored at all but only appeared so because it was under blue light, I could say: "It appeared
garish to me but really it was not," as long as "garish" is used in some
fairly stable group and is not merely a private word which I use in
some special idiosyncratic sense of my own.

The first step in handling Mrs. Hungerland's argument must be to
draw the teeth of her contention that the seems-is distinction when
applied to aesthetic terms is metaphoric only. To do this, let us first
review her criteria for non-metaphoric cases. They are: (1) that we can
establish what it is to be a *normal observer*, and (2) that we can establish
normal perceptual conditions, the former being constituted by absence
of physical defects in sense organs, the latter by "physical viewpoint,

---

[10] Perhaps one tends to say "I seem to have a headache" when reporting a mild headache,
and "I have a headache" when reporting a more severe one. Of course there are senses in
which we can say "I seem to have a headache but really I don't," but they are in unusual
circumstances, for example: if I am pretending to have a headache – rubbing my head,
groaning, etc. – and then let you know that I am only pretending after all.

[11] *Ibid.*, p. 65.

lighting arrangements, and so on." These things we can of course do for color perception which, it will be recalled, is her paradigm.

But by these criteria who shall scape whipping? Take, for example, terms like "lazy" and "intelligent" which were our paradigms of condition-governed terms in the preceding chapters. Surely it makes perfect sense to say "He appears lazy (or intelligent) but really he isn't." Are these literal uses of the seems-is distinction? Or are they metaphoric extensions? By Mrs. Hungerland's criteria I should think we would have to say that they are metaphoric. For there is certainly no special sense organ by which we recognize laziness or intelligence and which we can examine for defects. Nor is there some special set of optimal conditions for observing laziness or intelligence over and above the optimal conditions for observing *anything*. Are we then to conclude that we speak metaphorically when we say "He appears lazy (or intelligent) but really he isn't"? Have we been speaking metaphorically all of our lives without knowing it? It is hard to swallow. But grant that much of the seems-is distinction for aesthetic terms as is applicable to ordinary condition-governed terms like "lazy" and "intelligent" and I have established my case. The question is, Can that much be granted? It is here that the rest of Mrs. Hungerland's argument must be confronted.

The claim that color terms help establish our "public," "objective" world is of course true. And it is true too that aesthetic terms of various kinds are "variable" in a way that color terms are not. But we must ask ourselves, as in the previous discussion, whether the taking of color terms as a paradigm will rule out application of the seems-is distinction to perfectly ordinary cases like "lazy" and "intelligent."

In attempting to answer this question, let me introduce at this point an instructive example of Mrs. Hungerland's. She writes:

If I am inclined to think that my apprehension of aesthetic effect is idiosyncratic, or that, for me, the effect has no stability, I shall be inclined to treat my statement as though it were a *looks (to me now)* statement. But if I am a member of a coterie or am hardened in one of the current snobberies of the radicals or conservatives in art, I shall be inclined to treat my statement more like a *This is N* statement, and summon – if challenged – other "normal" observers to look at it as I do, from a "normal" viewpoint. So far, the metaphor works. But a rebel from within, or a Philistine from without, may dispute my standards of "normality." Time and again the rebel or the Philistine has partly or wholly prevailed, in that, partly owing to his efforts, we begin to apprehend different A's in the same object.[12]

[12] *Ibid.*, p. 58.

It is perfectly clear, and no one would want to deny, that the situation represented in this example stands in sharp contrast to the situation we are in when we pronounce objects "red," "blue," or whatever. No rebel from within or Philistine from without can question the standards of normal perception that help to make color part of our common "objective" world. But again, is it not misleading to choose color perception as our paradigm? Do concepts like "laziness" or "intelligence" constitute our public "objective" world or not? Certainly there are no standards of normal perception in these cases except the ones that are standard for *all* perception: sound mind, properly functioning senses, acceptable conditions for observing. And no rebel or Philistine can question *them*. Yet there is a sense in which the world of lazy and intelligent men is not the "common" world of red barns and black beetles. Every man in Tahiti is lazy to the New Yorker, and every New Yorker phrenetic to the Tahitian. Intelligence too is to a certain degree culture-dependent in a way in which redness and blackness are not. Nor do rebels and Philistines give their attention only to aesthetic terms. Through their offices we do come to apprehend people as, for example, lazy or intelligent whom we did not apprehend that way before, not because we see something that we previously missed but because our "sensibilities," if you will, have undergone some kind of change. Our criteria change: p-making features are added and dropped, all within the framework of a condition-governed model for which the seems-is distinction is quite valid. To say that the seems-is distinction is valid for such terms as "lazy" and "intelligent" is not to say that our criteria of laziness and intelligence are immutable or even *as* immutable as our standards for color perception.

If the argument in the preceding chapters was good, we can say the same for aesthetic terms. Many – I will not say all – changes in what we might call our aesthetic sensibilities can be represented logically as changes in our criteria: p-making features are added and dropped, where p's are aesthetic terms. I say represented "logically" because this is not intended to be a description of what it "feels like" to cease to see something aesthetically as p or to come to see it that way. This is the logic, not the psychology of aesthetic sensibility. And it can accommodate changes in sensibility, rebels from within, Philistines from without, on a condition-governed model. Why, then, need we be loath to apply the seems-is distinction here even though it commonly accompanies other condition-governed terms?

J. L. Austin once recommended we "forget for a while about the beautiful and get down instead to the dainty and the dumpy."[13] Now aesthetic words like "dainty," and "dumpy" – to which we can add numberless others, "delicate," "graceful," and so on – are, as Sibley quite correctly observes, "in regular use in everyday discourse." There is nothing about them that suggests privacy, subjectivity, idiosyncracy. They help carve out our public world as much (or as little) as do concepts like "laziness" or "intelligence." The controlling group of all of these – the group that establishes normal usage – is the cultural group.

But let us take some more critically interesting aesthetic terms: for example, "unified" and "expressive." These, unlike "dainty" and "dumpy," are surely not on the tip of everyone's tongue. They are not diffused through a culture the way "intelligent," "lazy," "delicate" and "graceful" are. Yet even here there is nothing to suggest isolated cliques and private meanings. One learns to use "unified" and "expressive" (in their aesthetic contexts) when one becomes a member of a not very exclusive linguistic circle: the society of those who are interested enough in art or the "aesthetic" to do some talking about it. Thus, although the group which determines normal usage for "unified" and "expressive" is not so large a one as the cultural group which determines the normal use of "intelligent," "lazy," "dainty," and "dumpy," it is not by any means a private clique either.

When, then, does the group controlling normal use of an aesthetic term become so small that the term can no longer be considered "public"? (For that is really what it comes down to.) Obviously, this is not a question that can be answered with any exactitude.[14] But the asking of it can help us to see aesthetic terms in a more dynamic context, and keep us from putting them all in the same logical bag. There was a time when terms like "hot," "cool," and "square" were used by small coteries of musicians in quite private conspiratorial ways. These terms have passed into a more public use; and a term like "groovy" is now in about the same position they once were. Somewhere in the history of a term, be it aesthetic, or what you will, it may pass from private to public use, from coterie to cultural group. No one can say exactly when the change occurs anymore than one can tell what penny makes a man rich or which hair makes him bald. Surely not all aesthetic terms are in the public domain, and many may be

[13] J. L. Austin, "A Plea for Excuses," reprinted in *Philosophical Papers*, ed. J. O. Urmson and G. J. Warnock (London: Oxford University Press, 1961), p. 131.
[14] Cf. F. N. Sibley and Michael Tanner, "Objectivity and Aesthetics," *Proceedings of the Aristotelian Society*, Supplementary Volume, LXII (1968).

in the grey borderline area. Those that are not public are indeed unamenable to the seems-is distinction. But many are as public as any of the other condition-governed terms in ordinary language, and as amenable as they to the distinction between being and appearing.

Mrs. Hungerland, as we have seen, lays down two requirements for the metaphoric extension of "really is, not just appears" to an aesthetic term: (a) that the nonaesthetic qualities in virtue of which the aesthetic one is being ascribed are really present (and do not just appear to be); and (b) that there be some kind of substantial permanent public group-use of the term in question. There are two things to be said about these requirements: first, that they are not just requirements for aesthetic terms but can be generalized for any condition-governed term in ordinary language; second, that *therefore* it is highly misleading to call this a metaphoric extension: it is the genuine article. If I called Mr. A lazy or intelligent in virtue of his being p, q, and r (p, q, and r being the only lazy- or intelligent-making features that Mr. A had), one requirement of Mr. A's *really* being lazy or intelligent and not just seeming so would be that Mr. A really did in fact have features p, q, and r, and didn't just seem to have them. Another requirement would of course be that "lazy" and "intelligent" have a permanent community use. Why then should we call this a metaphoric extension, considering the immense number of terms in ordinary language that function in just the same way as "lazy" and "intelligent"? And why should we call it a metaphoric extension when the very same requirements hold for an aesthetic term? The question of metaphoric extension aside, though, all that a condition-governed model of aesthetic terms requires is the same status with respect to the seems-is distinction as "lazy," "intelligent," and other such garden-variety condition-governed terms. That, I think, it cannot be denied. If we are to fault the condition-governed model of aesthetic terms on the grounds that these terms are not amenable to the seems-is distinction, we will have to find arguments more compelling than Mrs. Hungerland's.

The Doctrine of Aesthetic Vision

Since the end of the eighteenth century, there has been a view widely held by thinkers of varying other persuasions that aesthetic perception is not ordinary perception of some special species of quality, but, rather, a special species of perception of ordinary qualities. This view, which has sometimes been called the doctrine of "aesthetic disinterestedness," had its beginnings at the outset of the eighteenth century – at the time, in fact, when aesthetics as we now think of it was first being practiced.[15] The crux of the doctrine is that what is distinctive about aesthetic perception arises from a particular attitude which we assume when we contemplate anything aesthetically.

The many convolutions of the doctrine as it passed through eighteenth-century British psychology and nineteenth-century German metaphysics led always away from the "reality" of the perceptual object. Early in the eighteenth century Francis Hutcheson emphasized the irrelevance, even the necessary absence of self-interest in the aesthetic attitude. The "Pleasure of Beauty," he wrote, "... is distinct from that Joy which arises from Self-love upon prospect of Advantage."[16] From the notion that aesthetic contemplation ignores the personal utility of the object contemplated comes the related notion that the aesthetic attitude is one of complete indifference to *possession* of the object. For what one need not use "upon prospect of Advantage," one need not bring home and lock away. And it is this aspect of aesthetic contemplation that Edmund Burke dwelt upon at mid-century:

> By beauty I mean, that quality or those qualities in bodies by which they cause love, or some passion similar to it. ... I likewise distinguish love, by which I mean that satisfaction which arises to the mind upon contemplating anything beautiful, of whatsoever nature it may be, from desire or lust; which is an energy of the mind, that hurries us on to the *possession* of certain objects that do not affect us as they are beautiful, but by means altogether different.[17]

Utility, and desire for the possession of the object having been declared irrelevant to the aesthetic attitude, it is but a step to the Kantian dictum that in aesthetic contemplation the *actual existence* of the object is a matter of complete indifference. Thus:

> The delight which we connect with the representation of the real existence of an object is called interest. ... Now where the question is whether something is beautiful, we do not want to know, whether we, or any one else, are, or even could be, concerned in the real existence of the thing, but rather what estimate we form of it on mere contemplation (intuition or reflection).[18]

---

[15] The story of aesthetic disinterestedness in the eighteenth century has been admirably told by Jerome Stolnitz in "On the Origins of 'Aesthetic Disinterestedness'," *Journal of Aesthetics and Art Criticism*, XX (1961).

[16] Francis Hutcheson, *An Inquiry into the Original of our Ideas of Beauty and Virtue* (2nd ed.; London, 1726), p. 12.

[17] Edmund Burke, *A Philosophical Enquiry into the Origin of our Ideas of the Sublime and Beautiful*, ed. J. T. Boulton (New York: Columbia University Press, 1958), p. 91. My italics.

[18] Immanuel Kant, *Critique of Aesthetic Judgement*, trans. J. C. Meredith (London: Oxford University Press, 1911), pp. 42–43.

We need trace the doctrine no further to extract the general argument with which we must deal; all of the necessary materials are in Kant's formulation. Kant, of course, like Hutcheson and Burke, is speaking here only of the beautiful. But if we generalize for aesthetic perception as a whole, we see that the reality of the object of aesthetic perception suffers the same fate: complete irrelevance. Hence it follows that when we describe an object aesthetically, our description need not be accurate: the object need not actually exist as described or indeed exist at all. When we describe an object aesthetically, we will describe it as p, q, and r if it appears p, q, and r, whether or not it is p, q, and r at all, or whether there is even an object appearing. In other words, it is sufficient for something being aesthetically p, q, and r that I am having p-ish, q-ish, and r-ish perceptions. So the distinction between being or only seeming aesthetically p, q, and r cannot arise; for something will be aesthetically p, q, and r when there are p-ish, q-ish, and r-ish appearances, irrespective of whether anything is p, q, and r at all. And if this is the case, then the condition-governed model of aesthetic terms cannot be correct: for one of its consequences is that it does indeed make sense to distinguish in an aesthetic description between being p, q, and r, and only appearing p, q, and r. If, therefore, we are to sustain the condition-governed model, we must dispatch, or at least disarm this well-entrenched adversary. And as the purpose here is not historical, it will be well to tangle rather with a contemporary embodiment, the most recent and most interesting being that of Vincent Tomas in a widely discussed article called "Aesthetic Vision."[19]

It is Tomas' aim to formulate a distinction between "ordinary vision" and "aesthetic vision," between seeing things in "the common way" and seeing things aesthetically. Roughly, the distinction is as follows:

(1) When we see things in "the common way," our attention is directed toward the stimulus objects that appear to us, or toward what they signify, and we do not particularly notice the ways in which these objects appear. . . .
(2) When we see things aesthetically, our attention is directed toward appearances, and we do not particularly notice the thing that presents the appearance, nor do we care what, if anything, it is that appears.[20]

Tomas illustrates the distinction with numerous examples, not, one suspects, all really illustrative of the same distinction, but one of which, at least for our purposes, can be taken as about typical.

---

[19] Vincent Tomas, "Aesthetic Vision," *The Philosophical Review*, LXVIII (1959).
[20] *Ibid.*, p. 53.

Commonly, when we see a penny, we are about to pay a bill or count our change, and it makes no difference to us how the penny looks. ... our attention is directed toward the stimulus object – as it "really is" – not toward its appearance. ... And if, for some reason, we are then asked, "How did it look?" we would probably reply, "Why – like a penny." But a penny may look dull or look shiny. Under some conditions it will look round, and under most conditions it will look elliptical. ... The reply, "It looks like a penny," is an indication that the penny was seen in the common way – that the perceiver did not notice the way the penny looked.[21]

The key concepts here, fraught with long-standing difficulties, are "appearance" and "stimulus object," which Tomas elsewhere calls "phenomenological object" and "ontological object."[22] It would be well to consider briefly the manner in which these troublesome notions are put forward in the present instance. We are asked to entertain the following "experiment in the imagination":

It is the seventeenth century and we are somewhere in the Vatican, in a room where there are also two other men, a picture, and a mirror. One of the men is Velasquez and the other is Pope Innocent X. The picture is the one referred to in art catalogues as *Pope Innocent X* (National Gallery of Art, Washington). The visual apparatus of each man, the lighting conditions, and everything else are "normal."[23]

Consider now these six cases:

(1) Velasquez looks at the Pope and we say "He sees a man."
(2) Velasquez looks at *Pope Innocent X* and we say "He sees a picture."
(3) Velasquez looks at the Pope's reflection in the mirror and we say "He sees a mirror."
(4) Velasquez looks at the Pope and he says "I see a man."
(5) Velasquez looks at *Pope Innocent X* and he says "I see a man."
(6) Velasquez looks at the Pope's reflection in the mirror and he says "I see a man."

On the undoubtedly true assumption that our descriptions in (1), (2), and (3) of what Velasquez saw are correct, Velasquez' description of what he saw in (5) and (6) would seem to be incorrect. For in (5) Velasquez did not see a man at all but a picture; and in (6) he did not see a man either but a reflection in a mirror. But (5) and (6) are not incorrect if we assume Velasquez to be describing what Tomas calls the "ontological" or "stimulus object": "if he was describing not the picture but a way in which the picture appeared to him, his description, so far as it went, was not inaccurate and need not be misleading."[24]

21 *Ibid.*, pp. 54–55.
22 "The Concept of Expression in Art," reprinted in *Philosophy Looks at the Arts*, pp. 30–44, *passim*.
23 "Aesthetic Vision," p. 55.
24 *Ibid.*, p. 57.

Because "In principle, the appearance of a man and the appearance of a portrait of a man could be identical, in which case the accurate descriptions of each appearance would be identical." (The same argument, of course, applies *pari passu* to the reflection in the mirror.)

What Tomas means by an "ontological" or "stimulus object," then, is an "object" of the kind we refer to when we say that Velasquez sees a man in (1), that Velasquez sees a picture in (2), and that Velasquez sees a mirror in (3); and what Tomas means by "appearance" or "phenomenological object" is what Velasquez refers to in (5) and (6) when he says that he sees a man. And in this sense of "appearance," Tomas concludes that "In every case of aesthetic vision, what is attended to is an appearance, and the question of what actual object – a picture, a mirror, or a man – presents that appearance does not arise."[25] In other words, "the question of reality does not arise in *any* case of aesthetic vision...."

Animadversions on the "Doctrine"

Tomas' position has been very capably criticized in recent years by Frank Sibley and by Marshall Cohen in a symposium devoted to the aesthetic relevance of the being-seeming distinction.[26] Sibley was prepared to defend a rather drastic revision of Tomas' position whereas Cohen rejected it almost entirely. I have studied both with great profit, and have been influenced by many of their examples. However, I intend to take a rather different tack here; and although I want to acknowledge my debt, I do not want to suggest that either Sibley or Cohen would agree with what I am about to say.

There is, to begin with, very good reason to doubt that in all aesthetic perception we are always attending to what Tomas calls the "appearance" and never to the "stimulus object," assuming we can really make the distinction clear. So if it were indeed the case that all aesthetic seeing is as Tomas describes it, there would remain a vast territory of aesthetic perception in which his strictures would not apply and in which there would be no reason to doubt the relevance of the seems-is distinction. With regard to aesthetic seeing there may be some prima facie plausibility to Tomas' analysis; but with aesthetic hearing one already begins to squirm, and at (say) the experience of

[25] *Ibid.*, p. 58.
[26] Frank Sibley, "Aesthetics and the Looks of Things"; Marshall Cohen, "Appearance and the Aesthetic Attitude," *The Journal of Philosophy*, LVI (1959), pp. 905–26.

reading *David Copperfield*, the mind boggles. In what sense am I attending to an "appearance" when listening to a symphony and a "stimulus object" when a fire engine goes by? Whatever I hear, it is the same kind of thing in both cases, and I am at a loss really whether to call it "appearance" or "stimulus object." But I certainly know how to describe what I hear: a siren, concert A, the screech of tires, an oboe, a bell, a diminished seventh. Which is the "appearance" and which the "stimulus object"?

Thus Tomas' argument gives us no reason to believe that the being-appearing distinction is irrelevant anywhere but in visual aesthetic perception (which is, indeed, the only kind he claims to examine). But does it lend support to the contention even here? I want to grant, for the sake of argument, that in every case of aesthetic vision, that is, of aesthetic seeing, we are, as Tomas maintains, attending to the "appearance," never the "stimulus object." I want to argue that even so it is false that "the question of reality does not arise in *any* case of aesthetic vision." There is, it seems to me, a kind of Platonic fallacy at work here which is worth ferreting out.

Once it was fashionable for scientists to give popular lectures in which they revealed that a piece of wood only appears solid but really is made up of a great many tiny particles, in violent motion, and a great deal of "empty space." The line that Wittgenstein, and others, have taken with regard to this rather perplexing statement of the scientist is to claim he is misusing language – misusing the distinction between being solid and only appearing so. Wittgenstein says in the *Blue Book*:

> We have been told by popular scientists that the floor on which we stand is not solid, as it appears to common sense, as it has been discovered that the wood consists of particles filling space so thinly that it can almost be called empty. This is liable to perplex us, for in a way of course we know that the floor is solid, or that, if it isn't solid, this may be due to the wood being rotten but not to its being composed of electrons. To say, on this latter ground, that the floor is not solid is to misuse language.[27]

The term "real" does not take some ultimate Platonic object which the scientist has grasped and the rest of us have not. We do not have to wait for the physicist's final word on the ultimate constituents of matter before we determine that the piece of wood we are contemplat-

---

[27] Ludwig Wittgenstein, *The Blue and Brown Books* (New York: Harper Torchbooks, 1965), p. 45. The "argument" between the scientist and the common man is set out in what has become a classic analysis: L. Susan Stebbing, *Philosophy and the Physicist* (New York: Dover Publications, 1958), ch. 3.

ing is really solid. Oak is solid; balsa wood and rotten logs look solid enough but really are not. And we all know how to find out which is what.

What makes the physicist's statement so seductively plausible in its implausibility? Partly it is the mistaken Platonic conviction which many of us consciously or unconsciously share with the physicist that the word "real" has its meaning in virtue of reference to some hidden reality which we have gradually been getting closer to and which the physicist has at long last started from its lair. But that is not all: it is partly, too, that the physicist has behaved in a way quite like in some respects the way we behave when we make the determination "really is" or "only appears." The distinction between appearance and reality in ordinary usage is spelled out by familiar sets of routines: by operations commonly accepted. To find out if the wood is really solid or only appears so we kick it, or push it, or scrutinize it: we do something to it. To find out if a swatch of fabric is one color or another we compare it to something, or bring it out into the daylight, or hold it at a different angle: we go though some accepted routine. The physicist too, when he discovers that the wood is not really solid but a conjury of particles and spaces, goes through a routine: a particularly elaborate and fantastically sophisticated one; and *there* is where the trouble lies. For having gone through his routine as we have gone through ours, we feel that he has fulfilled the requirements which license one to conclude "only seems, really isn't." But not every routine will do. The ordinary meaning of "really solid" is limned in by a range of routines and operations to which the physicist's does not belong. This range is, one supposes, in some state of flux, and, no doubt, science has contributed to it over the centuries. However, until such time as this range expands to accommodate the procedures whereby the atomic physicist determines that the wood really isn't solid, he is indeed, as Wittgenstein says, misusing language, although he is misusing it in a way that is forever putting snares at our feet because of its parallel with ordinary linguistic usage.

Tomas makes the scientist's mistake of assuming that "real" does indeed name some ultimate object: in his case the "stimulus object." If he were correct, then anyone who is not dealing with the "stimulus object" cannot be dealing with the "real" but only the "appearance," and hence the question of reality cannot arise for him. But this is simply not the case. There are contexts in which the real is indeed the "stimulus object." There are, however, contexts in which the real is something else again, as in the following example. Suppose we are looking at a picture of a dress in the rotogravure section of the Sunday paper. I claim that the dress is fuchsia and you claim that it is violet, and we both agree on settling the matter through the commonly accepted routine of taking the picture out of doors and looking at it in direct sunlight. We do so and decide that it "really is" violet although it "looks" fuchsia in artificial light. But now along comes a third party who knows a little bit about printing and says: "You are both mistaken; the picture is neither fuchsia *nor* violet. It *looks* fuchsia in artificial light and violet in sunlight, if you scan it at a distance of a few inches; but if you examine it very closely you will see that it is *really* a mass of red and blue dots." Now you and I were truly discussing whether the dress is fuchsia or violet; but neither of us was talking about what Tomas calls the "stimulus object." We were talking about whether what Tomas calls the "appearance" really is fuchsia, or only appears so. And we settled the argument in a perfectly straightforward way without ever talking about the "stimulus object." It was only the third party, the printing expert, who was using "real" to refer to the "stimulus object" and "only seems" to refer to the "appearance," although he too made his determination through a common routine: "looking closely." Further, you and I and the third party were all using "really is" and "only seems" quite correctly; you and I were correct in concluding that the dress "really is" violet, and the third party was also correct when he concluded that the picture is neither fuchsia nor violet but "really" red and blue.

When the context and "routine" are such that the real is taken to be what Tomas calls the "stimulus object," then the dress cannot possibly be "really" fuchsia *or* violet; but in another context, and relative to another "routine," we may ask if the dress "really is" violet, and the answer may truthfully be "Yes." For the "stimulus object" is not the only "reality," the printer's scrutiny not the only "routine." Thus, even if the aesthetic object in aesthetic vision were never the "stimulus object" but always the "appearance," this would not *of itself* preclude our distinguishing in the aesthetic object between "really being" and "only appearing"; it would not *of itself* make the question of reality irrelevant.

However, this is not the whole story. For it may very well be sometimes true that the distinction between "really is "and "only appears" is indeed irrelevant in a given context or from a certain point of view.

Attending to the "appearance" rather than the "stimulus object," I have argued, does not render the distinction irrelevant. But there are other conditions, perhaps, that might. So it might be argued that these conditions – whatever they may be – always obtain when we are contemplating something aesthetically. The best way to deal with this argument, I think, is to find some context (not necessarily aesthetic) in which the distinction between being and appearing *is* irrelevant. For as it stands, the claim is a vague one and requires exemplification. Having done this, we can ask ourselves whether this context – and its relevant conditions – characterize all aesthetic perception.

Consider the old dispute about whether or not the pitcher's "curve ball" really curves or only appears to. Suppose it were determined by means of some photographic apparatus or other that Dizzy's curve ball really does curve but that Daffy's doesn't, being only an extremely convincing optical illusion. Suppose further that even after all of the batters are convinced by the photographic evidence, when Daffy throws his "curve ball" to the batter at the plate it still appears to the batter to curve, and no matter how he fights against them, his reflexes always react as if it really does curve, forcing him to swing where it isn't. From the batter's point of view Daffy's curve looks exactly like Dizzy's and is just as hard to hit, no matter how much the batter squints or tells himself "It doesn't really curve at all." Surely we could say that from the batter's point of view, the distinction between appearance and reality – between seeming to curve and really curving – is irrelevant. Dizzy can hardly ask for a higher salary than Daffy because his curve ball "really curves" and Daffy's does not – nor can the batters take any consolation in it. So here is a case in which from a certain point of view it is quite irrelevant whether something appears so-and-so or really is.

Is this the kind of situation we are *always* in when we contemplate things from the aesthetic point of view? It may very well be that it is sometimes irrelevant from the aesthetic point of view whether an object appears p or really is p. That there is no need to contest. But is it *always* irrelevant, from the aesthetic point of view? Of course knowing exactly *what the* aesthetic point of view is would, we justifiably feel, help considerably in answering this question. The trouble is, as we have seen, that the question "What is the aesthetic point of view?" often has had as its answer "The point of view from which it is irrelevant whether X is p or only appears p." So the thesis that the being-appearing distinction is always irrelevant in aesthetic perception becomes true by virtue of the irrelevance of the distinction becoming the defining property of aesthetic perception. Yet, without essaying our own answer to this much-vexed (and perhaps over-worked) question "What is the aesthetic point of view?" we can certainly point out that there seem to be cases in which we would (intuitively, at least) want to say: "Here is an instance of the aesthetic point of view in which the being-appearing distinction is relevant."

Let me illustrate with one kind of example where the distinction between being and appearing seems to play an essential role in an aesthetic context. The example is provided by Joshua Reynolds in the fourteenth of the *Discourses*:

> it is certain that all those odd scratches and marks, which, on close examination, are so observable in Gainsborough's pictures, and which even to experienced painters appear rather the effect of accident than design: this chaos, this uncouth and shapeless appearance, by a kind of magic, at a certain distance assumes form, and all the parts seem to drop into their proper places, so that we can hardly refuse acknowledging the full effect of diligence, under the appearance of chance and hasty negligence. That Gainsborough himself considered this peculiarity in his manner, and the power it possesses of exciting surprise, as a beauty in his works, I think may be inferred from the eager desire which we know he always expressed, that his pictures, at Exhibition, should be seen near, as well as at a distance.[28]

Notice that Reynolds distinguishes between appearance and reality here in what we might think of as a reversal of Tomas' usage. For it is "the odd scratches and marks" which, one would think, are Tomas' "stimulus object," and *they* are Reynold's "appearance," "this uncouth and shapeless appearance," whereas the "reality" is Tomas' "appearance," which only emerges at a distance, where "all the parts drop into their proper places, so that we can hardly refuse acknowledging the full effect of diligence, under the appearance of chance and hasty negligence." Or, to use Tomas' alternate terminology, the "ontological object" is Tomas' reality and Reynold's appearance, the "phenomenological object" Tomas' appearance and Reynold's reality. We have, then, not only a case in which the being-appearing distinction is aesthetically relevant, but a case in which the term "real" has reference to what Tomas would claim it cannot refer – the latter circumstance perhaps indicating what a slippery pair of customers "appearance" and "reality" really are.

But let us now turn Reynolds upside down and conform ourselves to

[28] Sir Joshua Reynolds, *Discourses*, ed. Edmund Gosse (London: Kegan Paul, Trench and Co., 1883), p. 263. Cf. E. H. Gombrich, *Art and Illusion* (2nd ed.; New York: Pantheon Books, 1965), pp. 191–202.

Tomas' terminology. For certainly there are a great many features that will "drop into their places" when we step back from a Gainsborough and that we might want to call "appearances" which the "stimulus object" ("those odd scratches and marks") presents: a mass of red and yellow scratches will become a smooth orange patch, aesthetic qualities such as "tension," "delicacy," "balance," and the rest, will emerge. We can thus say that the Gainsborough, from a certain distance, appears p, q, and r, where p, q, and r are a mixed bag of aesthetic and nonaesthetic qualities, but that when we examine the picture closely we find that it is not p, q, or r at all. Not only is this a perfectly correct way of using "is" and "appears," it is a vital part of the way we describe the Gainsborough aesthetically. It is not the case that all we are interested in here is how the Gainsborough appears from the viewing distance at which p, q, and r jump into place; we are interested too in the fact that it really isn't p, q, or r at all but only a collection of "scratches." Part of our aesthetic experience, of course, involves perceiving p, q, and r, but part of it too involves closer scrutiny of Gainsborough's jagged brush-strokes: "what we enjoy," writes E. H. Gombrich, "is not so much seeing these works from a distance as the very act of stepping back, as it were, and watching our imagination come into play, transforming the medley of color into a finished image."[29] This is a description of an aesthetic experience. Unlike the batter's point of view, the aesthetic point of view in this experience is not confined to a certain circumscribed place. Our aesthetic vantage point, in contemplating the Gainsborough, is not restricted to the viewing distance at which the "medley of colors" transforms itself into the "finished image." We are meant to step closer to a Gainsborough, just as we are meant to walk around a Rodin.

Consider, though, the following comment: "Those little colored scratches of the Gainsborough only appear to be solid little masses of color; if you look at them under a microscope you will see that they are *really* bits of pigment imbedded in drab blobs of linseed oil." The critic might here reply: "We are not interested, when we contemplate the Gainsborough aesthetically, in what the scratches really are – only in how they appear." So, it might be argued, when we view the Gainsborough from one foot away, and then from fifteen, we are not seeing first how things are and then how they appear; we are seeing how they appear from one foot away and how they appear from fifteen; only the microscope reveals what *really* is, and *that* is aesthetically irrelevant.

[29] *Art and Illusion*, p. 199.

Thus (the argument continues) we *are* only attending, in aesthetic contemplation, to how the Gainsborough appears, not what it really is.

How we reply to this argument depends upon whether or not we want to accept unchallenged the statement that the scratches of the Gainsborough only appear solid but (under the microscope) are revealed really to be grey blobs with color-flecks. Is this statement like the physicist's – that the wood really isn't solid but tiny particles and a lot of space? If so, then we can reply simply: it is a misuse of language and hence false to say that the scratches are not really solid masses of color. But if we want to accept the statement at face value, we must concede that there is nothing wrong with representing matters in this way. We must insist, however, that it is not the only correct way of representing them. What we see through the microscope has no monopoly on reality here: to claim that would be to commit the Platonic fallacy of thinking the "real" is some special object. There may be nothing wrong in saying that the Gainsborough appears *p*, *q*, and *r* from fifteen feet away, appears a medley of scratches from one foot away, and really is a collection of bits of pigment imbedded in grey linseed oil. But there is nothing wrong, either, in the critic saying that the Gainsborough appears *p*, *q*, and *r* from fifteen feet away, but when you get up close you discover that it really is a medley of color scratches. That this latter description is equally correct is adequate for the present purposes.

What might the upholder of "aesthetic vision" reply? Suppose that he insists the "aesthetic point of view" is only the point of view from which the Gainsborough *appears* *p*, *q*, and *r*. In a way, the phrase "aesthetic point of view," taken quite literally, suggests a certain place. And what is *the* aesthetic point of view – *the* specific place from which we view the Gainsborough aesthetically? (The batter's point of view, after all, is specifically given to be a marked off square in which he must stand.) It cannot be *both* fifteen feet away and one foot away if there is only *one* aesthetic point of view *literally*. Well, if it must be one or the other, what more reasonable conclusion than that the aesthetic point of view is the point fifteen feet from the picture where everything "falls into place," where the picture appears *p*, *q*, and *r*?

First, I think, we must resist taking the phrase "aesthetic point of view" literally. Second, we must ask why we should place the aesthetic point of view where the upholder of the doctrine of aesthetic vision would wish us to place it. If we insist that the aesthetic point of view must be the point of view from which the painting appears *p*, *q*, and *r*, then it merely becomes true by fiat – by stipulative definition – that from the aesthetic point of view only the appearance is attended to. But is the philosopher to legislate the aesthetic point of view solely for the protection of his pet theory? Gainsborough, Reynolds tells us, expressed "the eager desire that his pictures, at Exhibitition, should be seen near, as well as at a distance." Was Gainsborough *not*, then, expressing his wishes as to the aesthetic point of view his viewers should take? Is there a better way of describing what Gainsborough was expressing than to say that he was expressing his views about the aesthetic point of view proper to his pictures? If we give up this way of describing it, we should have compelling reasons for doing so; for if "aesthetic point of view" has any ordinary linguistic use at all, outside of aesthetic theories, here is that use – to characterize the way a painter thinks his pictures should be looked at.

If then, we substitute "aesthetic attitude" (say) for "aesthetic point of view," or if we take "aesthetic point of view" in other than a strictly literal sense, we can safely say that the aesthetic attitude, or aesthetic point of view, whatever else it may be, is an attitude or point of view which includes seeing the Gainsborough close up, far away, stepping back, and, in Gombrich's words "watching our imagination come into play, transforming the medley of color into a finished image." The aesthetic point of view is not one vantage point – like the batter's point of view, or a seat on the fifty-yard line. I may be taking the aesthetic point of view all the while I am walking forward and back, looking at the Gainsborough now from here, now from there. And from this complex "point of view" the distinction between what is and what appears is very relevant indeed.

There is, to be sure, a good deal more to the question than can be illustrated with this single example. It might rather be the subject of another book. For the present one, however, we must let the matter drop with the tentative conclusion that the irrelevance of the being-appearing distinction in *all* aesthetic contexts is, at least, very doubtful, and therefore must be given a Scotch verdict.

Recapitulation

I examined two arguments in this chapter which were supposed to show that aesthetic terms cannot be condition-governed. The first, which I called the *specific* argument, was that the logic of aesthetic terms excludes the distinction between appearance and reality; and that since if aesthetic terms were condition-governed, this would not be the case, aesthetic terms cannot be condition-governed. The second argument took its departure from a more general premise: that in aesthetic contemplation the question of reality is always irrelevant. From this premise it seemed to follow that the distinction between "really is" and "only seems" can never arise in aesthetic contemplation; and since the condition-governed model implies that it does indeed arise, the condition-governed model cannot be correct.

The general conclusion of this chapter was that neither of the arguments considered here provides anything conclusive in the way of ruling out the relevance of the seems-is distinction to aesthetic describing or aesthetic perceiving; and that the condition-governed model of aesthetic terms cannot be faulted on such grounds. I turn now to yet another strategy that might be employed to do the job which the present one has failed to do.

CHAPTER V

DUCK-RABBIT AND OTHER PERPLEXITIES

Aspects or Qualities?

Since quite early in the eighteenth century, perhaps even before, judgments of the form "X is beautiful" have seemed to many to occupy some kind of middle-ground between the "objective" and the "subjective" – the defensible and the merely idiosyncratic. One of its most interesting and little commented upon expressions occurs in Francis Hutcheson's first *Inquiry* (1725) where he writes in one place:

> by *Absolute* or *Original* Beauty, is not understood any Quality suppos'd to be in the Object, which should of itself be beautiful, without relation to any Mind which perceives it: For Beauty, like other Names of sensible Ideas, properly denotes the *Perception* of some Mind; so *Cold, Hot, Sweet, Bitter*, denote the Sensations in our Minds, to which perhaps there is no resemblance in the Objects, which excite these Ideas in us, however we generally imagine that there is something in the Object just like our Perception. The Ideas of Beauty and Harmony being excited upon our *Perception* of some *primary Quality*, and having relation to *Figure* and *Time*, may indeed have a nearer resemblance to Objects, than these Sensations, which seem not so much any *Pictures* of Objects, as *Modifications* of the perceiving Mind; and yet were there no mind with a *Sense* of Beauty to contemplate Objects, I see not how they could be call'd beautiful.[1]

Couched in terms of a derivative Lockean empiricism, we have here recognition on Hutcheson's part that there is something peculiarly "between the cracks" about judgments of the beautiful. The notorious "resemblance" theory of perception, which Locke's immediate followers and critics extracted, perhaps mistakenly, from the *Essay Concerning Human Understanding*, had it that such "sensations" as those of coldness, hotness, bitterness, sweetnesss, were mental entities taken (wrongly) as pictures or representations of qualities in the external world; whereas such "sensations" as those of shape, motion, and so on – the so-called "primary qualities" – *were* indeed "resemblances"

[1] Hutcheson, *Inquiry*, pp. 14–15.

of external qualities. If "X is square" be taken, then, as the paradigm case of an "objective" judgment, and "X is bitter" of a subjective one, what are we to say of a judgment that predicates p of X, where p names a "sensation" which bears "a nearer resemblance" to an external quality than the sensations of bitterness or sweetness do, but nevertheless names only a sensation – "properly denotes the *Perception* of some Mind" – just as "bitter" and "sweet"? It cannot be an "objective" judgment; for then p would name something in addition to a sensation, that is, a quality which the appropriate sensation resembles. Nor can it be a "subjective" judgment either; for then there could not be that "near" resemblance of the sensation to the quality: there could be no resemblance at all. Thus, albeit in an awkward theory, Hutcheson has expressed what to a host of aestheticians since has been an important truth about aesthetic value judgment: that it wavers between the subjective and the objective.[2]

It is this kind of hermaphroditic existence that has also seemed to many to characterize the terms we use to describe (rather than evaluate) works of art. And that, I suspect, is one of the reasons why the phenomenon known as "aspect-perceiving" has figured so prominently in recent discussions of aesthetic perception. I shall begin, where such discussions usually do, with a picture called the "Duck-Rabbit," which Wittgenstein was mainly responsible for projecting into philosophy in general, and, indirectly, into aesthetics in particular.

The figure can be "seen as" either a duck's or a rabbit's head.

Consider now, the following three "disagreements":

(1) Mr. A says the artichoke is bitter and Mr. B says it is sweet.
(2) Mr. A says the rose is red and Mr. B says it is blue.
(3) Mr. A says "It's a duck" and Mr. B says "It's a rabbit."

It would seem that (3) falls somewhere between (1) and (2). For (3) is something like (1) in that the figure is both a duck and a rabbit, duck

² In Kant's more familiar formulation, "the judgement of taste is ... one resting on subjective grounds ... which yet, for all of that, is objective ... ," *Critique of Aesthetic Judgement*, p. 70.

to Mr. A, rabbit to Mr. B, as the artichoke is both bitter and sweet, bitter to Mr. A and sweet to Mr. B; whereas it is unlike (2) in that the rose is not – cannot be – both red and blue. And (3) is, on the other hand, something like (2) and unlike (1) in that we feel being duck-like or rabbit-like are somehow "qualities" of the "object," as red or blue might be: that Mr. A and Mr. B are perceiving a different quality "in" the "object" when Mr. A sees it as a duck and Mr. B sees it as a rabbit; whereas they are not when the artichoke tastes bitter to Mr. A and sweet to Mr. B. Aspect-perceiving, if we mean by it the kind of thing the Duck-Rabbit represents, seems somehow to mediate between the subjective and the objective – much as Hutcheson conceived of the aesthetic value judgment – "between the cracks." Or, as Wittgenstein characteristically puts the matter: "'But this isn't seeing!' – 'But this is seeing!' – It must be possible to give both remarks a conceptual justification."[3]

It *seems*, then, that the logic of aspect-ascriptions is somewhere between that of condition-governed terms and that of purely subjective feeling-reports, yet far enough away from the logic of condition-governed terms to be non-condition-governed itself. Those who accept the view that aesthetic terms are non-condition-governed tend also, therefore, to look with favor on the view that aesthetic perceiving is aspect-perceiving. It saves the appearance of non-condition-governed behavior and, at the same time, does not fly into the arms of out-and-out subjectivism. Now if all aesthetic ascribing is aspect-ascribing – if when we ascribe p to X, where p is an aesthetic term, we are really ascribing p as an aspect – it follows that all aesthetic ascribing is non-condition-governed. But if aspect-ascribing is non-condition-governed, and if all aesthetic ascribing is aspect-ascribing, our thesis is defeated: aesthetic terms cannot possibly be condition-governed.

How may we defend our thesis against this argument? Two avenues lie open. We can attack the claim that all aesthetic perceiving is aspect-perceiving; or we can attack the claim that aspect-terms are non-condition-governed. For if all aesthetic perceiving is not aspect-perceiving, there is no reason to believe that all aesthetic ascribing is aspect-ascribing, and, therefore, no reason to believe that all aesthetic ascribing is non-condition-governed even *if* all aspect-ascribing is. And even if all aesthetic perceiving *were* aspect-perceiving, if aspect-ascribing were condition-governed, our thesis would be saved: aesthetic

[3] Ludwig Wittgenstein, *Philosophical Investigations*, trans. G. E. M. Anscombe (New York: Macmillan, 1953), p. 203e.

terms would be aspect-terms, but condition-governed for all of that. I shall attack on both fronts. In the next section I want to argue that all aesthetic perceiving is *not* aspect-perceiving; and in the one following that at least some aspect-ascribing is condition-governed.

Aspect-Perceiving and Aesthetic Perceiving

We spoke in the chapter preceding of a long-standing program in aesthetics, namely, the attempt to understand aesthetic perceiving not as ordinary perceiving of extraordinary qualities but, rather, as a special way of perceiving ordinary qualities. That program is being perpetuated still in the recent attempts to construe aesthetic perceiving as aspect-perceiving. There has been more than one such attempt: the thing is definitely in the air. It would be impossible, within the confines of the present study, however, to canvas the field. I shall therefore concentrate on one formulation of the view, that of B. R. Tilghman in a recent essay called "Aesthetic Perception and the Problem of the 'Aesthetic Object'." This places a severe but, I am afraid, a necessary limitation on my argument here. For my aim, as originally stated, was to show that: (1) all aesthetic perceiving is not aspect-perceiving; and that (2) therefore even *if* aspect-ascriptions are not condition-governed, it does not follow that aesthetic ascriptions are not condition-governed. However, establishing that one particular view of aesthetic aspect-perceiving is mistaken will not establish that all such views are mistaken; will not, that is, establish (1). All that I can hope to do here is cast some doubt on the view that aesthetic perceiving is aspect-perceiving by refuting the view in one of its formulations, and by doing that give some support – but by no means overwhelming support – to the conclusion that the non-condition-governed behavior of aspect-ascribing does not imply the non-condition-governed behavior of aesthetic terms.

Tilghman takes his departure, as I have, from Wittgenstein's discussion of the Duck-Rabbit. And he points out, as Wittgenstein did, that when we have come to see the ambiguous nature of the figure, we have come to see something in quite a different way than a person who as yet only sees "a duck" or "a rabbit." To begin with, a person who only sees "a duck," or "a rabbit," would not think of saying "I am seeing it *as* a duck," or "I am seeing it *as* a rabbit": only, "It's a duck," or "It's a rabbit." "It would make no sense for the man who had seen only the rabbit-aspect to say 'I am seeing it as a rabbit'."

But when one comes to see both the duck- and the rabbit-aspect ot the Duck-Rabbit,

> he may also realize that in both instances he was seeing the same object and that in reality the figure is neither a duck nor a rabbit, but a duck-rabbit that can be seen now as the one and now as the other. He may even notice the change taking place, as it were, before his eyes and he can say "Now it is a duck and now it is a rabbit."[4]

What are the significant characteristics of this new way of seeing not just a duck or a rabbit but a duck-rabbit, now *as* a duck, now *as* a rabbit? Tilghman writes:

> I take it that to report a perception is to report that an object of a certain sort is seen. Thus, I report seeing a rabbit-figure, the duck-rabbit figure, or, not being aware of the visually ambiguous character of the duck-rabbit, that I see another rabbit-figure. But when I notice the ambiguous character of the duck-rabbit and see it now as a duck and then as a rabbit and say "Now it's a rabbit" I am not reporting a perception. That is, I am not reporting that I am seeing a different object. The object remains the same, I see it is the same and has not changed, but yet I see it in a different way.[5]

Thus, when we have come to see the Duck-Rabbit now as a duck, now as a rabbit, we have come to see "something" which changes and yet does not change. Were we reporting a "perception" when we said first "Now it's a duck," and then "Now it's a rabbit," we would be reporting that something had changed from a duck into a rabbit (or a duck had been replaced by a rabbit). But when we report "Now I see it as a duck," and then "Now I see it as a rabbit," we are clearly not reporting a change in the figure: "it is a report that I have seen the object in a new way."

Seeing now the duck, now the rabbit, requires, of course, that one have a normally functioning perceptual apparatus; but it requires too achieving a certain technique: a perceptual skill of a distinctive sort. "The logic of seeing-as necessarily involves the notion of the mastery of techniques in addition to any possibly necessary physiological conditions."[6] One must, to begin with, be acquainted with ducks and rabbits – which, to be sure, is a prerequisite also for recognizing non-ambiguous pictures of ducks and rabbits. Beyond that, though, "Seeing the figure as a duck involves the ability to do such things as describe the figure as one would a real duck, e.g. point out the relevant

---

[4] B. R. Tilghman, "Aesthetic Perception and the Problem of the 'Aesthetic Object'," *Mind*, New Series, LXXV (1966), p. 359.

[5] *Ibid.*, p. 360.

[6] *Ibid.*, p. 362.

features of the head, show which way it is looking, etc.; match the figure with a picture of a real duck, and the like."[7] The same kind of ability is involved, of course, in seeing the figure as a rabbit. And, one presumes, being able to see the figure as a duck *or* a rabbit requires both the duck-skills, the rabbit-skills, as well as the achievement of seeing the figure now as one, now as the other – an achievement which cannot simply be the sum of the other two.

At this point Tilghman is prepared to apply the notion of aspect-perceiving to aesthetic perception. But before we follow him in this it would be well to pause for a moment and meditate on the strategy that must be employed in taking the step from the Duck-Rabbit to the work of art.

J. L. Austin has pointed out that there are many ways of describing "seeing" in ordinary language, "different ways of saying what is seen," which can be described too in terms of "seeing as."[8] Thus, to say that aesthetic perception is a case of "seeing as" may be to say nothing more than that aesthetic perception is a case of perception, since "seeing as" may simply be another way to describe perfectly ordinary ways of perceiving. In order for the statement "Aesthetic perception is a case of 'seeing as'" to be made informative and non-trivial, we must unpack the notion of "seeing as" embodied in it. There is nothing trivial in the statement "Seeing the Duck-Rabbit now as a duck, now as a rabbit, is a case of 'seeing as .'" But that is because one has spelled out how this particular kind of "seeing as" differs from ordinary seeing. The same must be done for the former statement; and this, as we shall see, leads to difficulties.

The transition from perceiving the Duck-Rabbit to perceiving a work of art aesthetically is made by Tilghman with the following example.

Imagine someone looking at the shop drawings of a piece of machinery. To a layman or an engineer unfamiliar with that particular mechanism the drawings might appear to be a confused jumble of lines. The trained engineer, however, may come to see the drawing as a certain piece of machinery. The lines now fall into their proper relationships and he recognizes the various parts of the mechanism and how they fit together.[9]

Perceiving a painting, for example, like perceiving the blueprint, is a case of either seeing or not seeing things "fall into their proper re-

---

[7] *Ibid.*, p. 361.
[8] J. L. Austin, *Sense and Sensibilia*, ed. G. J. Warnock (New York: Oxford University Press, 1964), p. 101.
[9] Tilghman, *op. cit.*, pp. 362–63.

lationships"; seeing or not seeing "how they fit together." To see things "in their proper place," to see "how they fit together" in a painting is to see the painting aesthetically. "When we appreciate a painting we come to see the elements of line, shape, and colour as hanging together in a coherent design and we come to see the human and emotional significance of the scenes represented." Thus we now have our required analysis of aesthetic "seeing as": it is a kind of *appreciation* in which we perceive things as hanging together, as coherent; and we see "human and emotional significance."

Now there are, it seems to me, two very obvious and fatal kinds of counterexample that can be adduced here. First, let us imagine someone listening rather dreamily, and perhaps not too intently, to the lilting and seductive strains of Weber's *Invitation to the Dance*. He seems to be having a pleasant enough experience. But along comes a musician to disturb his revery and educate his perception. "Notice," the musician says, "that this is not merely a string of waltzes. It is a *rondo* in which one of the waltzes recurs, setting up a pattern of repetition. (Weber in fact subtitled it *Rondeau brillant*.) Further, the work is introduced by a seemingly diffuse section which, however, has a definite program:

First approach of the dancer to whom the lady gives an evasive answer. His more pressing invitation; her acceptance of his request. Now they converse in greater detail; he begins; she answers; he with heightened expression; she responds more warmly; now for the dance! His remarks concerning it; her answer; their coming together; their going forward; expectation of the beginning of the dance.[10]

And it ends with a coda, also programatic, which utilizes the same thematic material as the introduction. A perfectly rounded musical form!" At once the piece is seen by the previously casual listener to "hang together"; he comes to see, too, "the human and emotional significance represented."

But now a problem arises. We would all agree that before the musician came along to instruct him, our listener was not having a particularly deep or rich experience; but he was having an *aesthetic* experience, albeit a shallow and undistinguished one. Yet the work was not seen by him to "hang together," nor did he see its emotional and human significance. It would certainly be odd to insist that his experience of *Invitation to the Dance* was, prior to instruction, not an aesthetic experience. If that wasn't an aesthetic experience, what was

[10] John Warrack, *Carl Maria von Weber* (New York: Macmillan, 1968), p. 191.

it? Nevertheless, it was an experience, in which what was being perceived was *not* perceived as "hanging together," was *not* perceived as emotionally and humanly significant. So it couldn't, according to Tilghman, be a case of aesthetic perception; it couldn't be an aesthetic experience.

Of course one can always stubbornly insist that the work does *really* seem to the listener to "hang together" and is *really* perceived as emotionally and humanly significant even before the musician happens along, but "hangs together" in a *different* way and has *different* emotive and human significance before the listener has been enlightened. But this sounds very much like bending the facts to fit the theory. If "hanging together" and "seeing emotional and human significance" mean what they ordinarily do, then, I submit, our example is a very clear case of coming to see something "hanging together," and coming to see it as emotionally and humanly significant when previously it was not seen so. Conversely, one can stubbornly insist that the pre-instruction perception is not *really* aesthetic, but, again, at the cost of subjecting the facts to the theory, in the manner of the man who insists "This couldn't be pudding because I like it – and I don't like pudding."

The second counterexample arises from Tilghman's apparent identification of aesthetic perception with a kind of *appreciation*. For consider the following case. Mr. A is reading a novel. He neither likes the novel nor does he think it is a good novel; in fact he finds it a bore and thinks it is trash. Can he correctly be described as "appreciating" the novel? Such a description would be strange in this context. Someone might be said to "appreciate" a novel that he was enjoying but thought was bad; and might be said to "appreciate" a novel that he did not like but thought was good.[11] He could hardly be said to "appreciate" a novel he neither liked nor thought was good. If he is not appreciating it, however, he cannot, according to Tilghman, be perceiving it aesthetically; for aesthetic perception, according to him, is a species of appreciating, and Mr. A is not appreciating the novel. So it follows from Tilghman's position that a person who is perceiving a work of art that he does not like and thinks is bad cannot be perceiving it aesthetically. But how, one wonders, can one find out if he enjoys a work of art and if it is a bad work of art except by perceiving it aesthetically? In a word, Tilghman's view simply cannot accommodate unpleasant

---

[11] I am assuming that it makes sense to say of a novel (or other work of art) "It's good but I don't like it," or 'It's bad but I like it."

experiences of bad works of art, at least it cannot accommodate them as "aesthetic" experiences – which seems to me to be an absolutely fatal flaw.

Tilghman's use of "appreciation" might, perhaps, be defended along the following lines.[12] Since we can say, for example, "He does not appreciate Hume's argument," meaning "He does not understand Hume's argument," we might sometimes mean "He does not understand Goethe's *Faust*" when we say "He does not appreciate Goethe's *Faust*." And if "appreciate" is taken in this way, then, presumably, it would make sense to say "He does not like Goethe's *Faust* and thinks it is a bad work of art, but he *appreciates* it." The trouble with this line of argument is that what we mean when we say "He does not understand Hume's argument" is not the same kind of thing we mean when we say "He does not understand Goethe's *Faust*"; and what we mean when we say "He does not appreciate Hume's argument" is not the same kind of thing we mean when we say "He does not appreciate Goethe's *Faust*." The following illustration may be helpful here:

Mr. A. I don't understand Beethoven's *Grosse Fuge*.
Mr. B. There is nothing to *understand*: you can understand an argument in Hume's *Treatise* but you can't understand the *Grosse Fuge*; it doesn't *say* anything.
Mr. A. You are taking "understand" in too literal a sense: when someone says they don't *understand* a work of art they don't mean it in the same way as when they say they don't understand a philosophical argument; they mean something like – well – *appreciate*.

In other words, in aesthetic contexts, "understand" is a somewhat figurative term which is more literally rendered by "appreciate"; and in (say) a philosophical context "appreciate" is a somewhat figurative term which is more literally rendered by "understand." To say "I understand Goethe's *Faust* but don't like it and think it is a bad work of art" is indeed an odd statement, in need of some kind of explanation, such as: "I don't mean *understand* in its usual aesthetic sense but, rather, in the sense in which I would say I don't *understand* Hume's arguments in the *Treatise*."

Thus our conclusion regarding Tilghman's identification of aesthetic perception with appreciation still stands. On Tilghman's view, unpleasant experiences of bad works of art cannot properly be called "aesthetic" experiences – sufficient grounds, one would think, for rejecting the view out of hand.

An interesting point emerges, I think, from Tilghman's attempt to

[12] This objection was raised by Elmer H. Duncan.

understand aesthetic perception as a kind of aspect-perceiving; and to bring it out more effectively I would like to sketch, very briefly, another possible approach to the same problem, an approach *suggested* by some remarks of Virgil Aldrich. I underscore the word "suggested" because the approach is one that I suspect Professor Aldrich would disavow, although the remarks I have in mind have served me as a springboard to it. Aldrich writes, in partial explanation of his claim that aspect-perceiving provides the key to aesthetic perception:

Let us call "observation" the perceptual mode in which material things are realized in physical space. Then the very looking at things will be an incipient awareness of their space properties as fixed by metrical standards and measuring operations. Things seen this way will have a different structural cast from that of the same things in the aesthetic perception of them. Let us call the latter mode "prehension." The aesthetic space of things perceived thus is determined by such characteristics as intensities of values of colors and sounds, which ... comprise the medium presented by the material things in question. ... Thus prehension is, if you like, an "impressionistic" way of looking, but still a mode of perception, with the impressions objectively animating the material things – there to be prehended.[13]

When we *observe*, in Aldrich's sense, "the characteristics of the material thing are realized as 'qualities' that 'qualify' it ..."; but when we *prehend*, we are either "getting aesthetic space-values of the thing as structured simply by color and sound ...," or "seeing the thing as something that it is not thought really to be...."

What catches the eye, here, are such contrasts as that between "metrical standards," "measuring operations," and "intensities or values of colors and sounds"; between "'qualities' that 'qualify'" and "seeing the thing as something it is not thought really to be," "an 'impressionistic' way of looking." To the reader coming fresh from (say) Tomas' article on "Aesthetic Vision," or any of the other traditional "appearance" theories of aesthetic perception, this sounds very like the contrast between cases of seeing in which the question of reality is relevant and cases in which it is not. And the possibility then presents itself of understanding aspect-perceiving in aesthetics in terms of seeing things merely *as* appearances. Thus the view suggested by – but not, I repeat, imputed to – Aldrich is that aesthetic perceiving is aspect-perceiving of the kind in which only the appearance is attended to.

Now as this view is merely a reexpression of the old view that aes-

[13] Virgil C. Aldrich, *Philosophy of Art* (Englewood Cliffs, N.J.: Pretentice-Hall, 1963), p. 22.

thetic perception involves attending not to things "as they really are" but "merely to the way things appear," it is open to all of the objections raised previously against the earlier view; and they need not be repeated here. What I wish to bring out, however, is that a seemingly new path has turned out to lead right back into a familiar and well-trodden dead end. And if we look at Tilghman's position with this in mind we will see the very same thing. For one of the major operators there is the notion of "hanging together" – the notion that what distinguishes aesthetic perception is a kind of "organic unity" or "wholeness" not met with in ordinary ways of perceiving the world. It turns out, then, to be a reexpression in part of the well-known "organicist" theory, against which a serious objection can be brought.

It has long been apparent that not merely aesthetic perception but *all* perception tends to exhibit "wholeness" or "unity" which meets the organicist's aesthetic requirements. Strawson, among others, has pointed this out in a review of Harold Osborne's recent venture into the organic theory of aesthetic perception. He writes: "when one recognizes a person's face or a locality or any individual thing, for which aesthetic excellence is not claimed, one may well be noticing something that passes Mr. Osborne's test for organic wholeness: *i.e.* one sees it as a single individual, and the parts might look different away from the whole."[14] To which we might add, Mr. Osborne's requirements for organic unity are met not only by perceptions for which no aesthetic *excellence* is claimed but for which no *aesthetic* quality of any kind is claimed: that is, for which "nonaesthetic" is the proper description. Mr. Osborne replies that aesthetic unity is "different in kind" from the unity of ordinary perception;[15] and that may very well be so. But it is in itself an admission that the concept of unity alone cannot distinguish the perception of aesthetic excellence from other kinds of perception in which aesthetic excellence is not claimed; and the argument will show too that the concept of unity alone cannot distinguish aesthetic from nonaesthetic perception unless one is willing to say – as some indeed have said – that *all* perception is aesthetic. It is unity "plus". . . . And what the extra magic ingredient is the notion of unity alone cannot tell us.

The organicist then appears to be caught between Scylla and Charyb-

[14] P. F. Strawson (in a review of H. Osborne's *Theory of Beauty*), *Mind*, New Series LXIII (1954), p. 415.
[15] Harold Osborne, "Artistic Unity and Gestalt," *The Philosophical Quarterly*, XIV (1964), p. 225.

dis. If he construes "coherence," or its ilk, in anything like the ordinary way, there seem to be cases (as in our example of Weber's *Invitation to the Dance*) where we want to say something is an instance of the aesthetic, but is not "coherent." If, on the other hand, he construes "coherence" in a sense wide enough to include everything we would want to call aesthetic, he ends up by having to include literally *everything*, the nonaesthetic as well as the aesthetic. Thus, again, the "new way" of aspect-perceiving has led us back to a very old, and, I think, unacceptable way of dealing with the problem of aesthetic perception.

Nor can we console ourselves on this regard with anything like "well begun, half done." There might be a temptation to think that identifying aesthetic perception with aspect-perceiving – i.e. "seeing as" – is a major insight, and the failure of two attempts at distinguishing *aesthetic* aspect-perceiving from other possible kinds a minor setback in comparison. But this is a mistake. To say that aesthetic seeing is "seeing as" means next to nothing unless we can explain aesthetic "seeing as" into the bargain. We must realize here the force of Austin's observation that "seeing as" can be the name for some perfectly ordinary kinds of seeing. To say "I see the Duck-Rabbit as a duck" may be to describe a different kind of seeing than the kind described by the boy at the Zoo who stands in front of the Gorilla's cage and says "I see a Gorilla." But the man who says "I see *Death of a Salesman* as a tragedy" or "I see *The Origin of Species* as the most important book of the nineteenth century" is seeing *Death of a Salesman* or *The Origin of Species* in exactly the same way as the man who says simply *"Death of a Salesman* is a tragedy" or *"The Origin of Species* is the most important book of the nineteenth century." It is a philosophical task to distinguish aesthetic perceiving from other kinds. It may very well be the *same* task to distinguish aesthetic "seeing as" from other possible kinds since "seeing as" need not necessarily be anything but ordinary seeing. And that is why the contention that aesthetic seeing is "seeing as" may very well be trivial, and the failure to distinguish aesthetic "seeing as" from ordinary kinds as profound a failure as the continued failure of philosophers to distinguish aesthetic perception from perception in general.

The Logic of Aspect-Ascribing

So far, I have tried in this chapter to cast *some* doubt at least on the view that aesthetic perception is a species of seeing-as in any non-trivial sense – the purpose of this being to defeat the argument that (1) aesthetic perceiving is aspect-perceiving; (2) therefore, aesthetic ascribing is aspect-ascribing; (3) aspect-ascribing is non-condition-governed; (4) therefore aesthetic ascribing is non-condition-governed or, in other words, aesthetic terms are non-condition-governed. I want now to concentrate on the third premise of this argument. For if it can be shown that the logic of aspect-ascribing can be represented on a condition-governed model, that is, if the third premise can be shown to be false, the argument will fail even if the first premise be true, thus reinforcing the plausibility of a condition-governed model of aesthetic terms – which of course is my purpose.

But we are faced, at the outset, with a very sticky problem. For aspect-perceiving, seeing-as, is not just a single concept – it is a veritable battalion of them. As Wittgenstein realized, "There are here largely many interrelated phenomena and possible concepts."[16] And we cannot hope to cope with them all.

I shall take the Duck-Rabbit as my paradigm case. And I shall assume that we have some kind of intuitive notion of what other more complex examples belong to the same family. I shall raise the question What (if any) sense does it make to talk about *defending* such statements as "It's a duck," "It's a rabbit," "It can be seen as a duck," "It can be seen as a rabbit," and the like? If it can be shown that it makes the same kind of sense to talk about defending these aspect-ascriptions as it does to talk about defending such statements as "Mr. A is lazy," or "Mr. B is intelligent," it will be shown that the former are condition-governed. For the latter are defensible in virtue of their being condition-governed.

Let us begin with an analogy. To the claim of naive subjectivists that "X is beautiful" can be understood as "I like X" (or something of the kind), it has been replied that the *appearance*, at least, of aesthetic discourse does not bear this out. As Harold Osborne put the case recently:

We *do* behave differently in face of aesthetic disagreements from our easy acceptance of personal likes and dislikes for smells, tastes, etc. Not only philosophers but people in general tend to presuppose by their behaviour and reactions that there is a right and wrong in matters of aesthetic taste, to attach some sort of condemnation for lack of taste, and we feel a sort of discomfort if

---

[16] Wittgenstein, *Philosophical Investigations*, p. 199e.

a man of trained sensibility rejects our aesthetic judgements which we do not feel if he does not share our liking for mangoes or meddlars.[17]

Along similar lines, can we learn anything about aspect-ascribing from our discourse to suggest that it is not obviously non-condition-governed? I think that we can.

There is a very well-known scene in *Hamlet* in which Hamlet's madness (or feigned madness) is depicted, in part, through what is apparently an ancient pastime: seeing pictures in clouds, seeing clouds *as* this or that.[18]

Hamlet. Do you see yonder cloud that's almost in shape of a camel?
Polonius. By th'mass and 'tis like a camel indeed.
Hamlet. Methinks it is like a weasel.
Polonius. It is backed like a weasel.
Hamlet. Or like a whale.
Polonius. Very like a whale.

Polonius, clearly, is humoring what he takes to be a madman. (At least that is the way the scene is usually played.) But *why* does he take Hamlet for mad? There is nothing mad about seeing a cloud as a camel, or a weasel, or a whale. There may, however, be something not quite right about seeing the *same* cloud at the *same* time as a camel, a weasel, and a whale. Here, it is suggested, the line has been crossed between seeing things in clouds and "seeing things"; between aspect-perceiving and hallucinating. Our discourse about aspects suggests then that there *is* such a line; and if there is, there must be criteria for determining when it has been crossed – in other words, criteria for determining whether or not a given figure can be rightly said to bear a certain aspect. What might these criteria be?

I will take my departure, here, from one of those pregnant remarks of Wittgenstein's which, like the pre-Socratic fragments, seem so easy to accommodate to whatever view the commentator is trying to support. (But this is a philosophical sport so wide-spread nowadays that, I suppose, it hardly requires an apology anymore.) The remark I have in mind is apropos of a drawing reproduced below:

[17] H. Osborne, "Wittgenstein On Aesthetics," *The British Journal of Aesthetics*, VI (1966), p. 386.
[18] Act III; scene ii.

Wittgenstein writes of this figure:

What tells us that someone is seeing the drawing three-dimensionally is a
certain kind of "knowing one's way about." Certain gestures, for instance,
which indicate the three-dimensional relations: fine shades of behaviour.[19]

I think what he has to say of it applies as well to the Duck-Rabbit.
To paraphrase the passage, what tells us that someone is seeing the
Duck-Rabbit as a duck or as a rabbit or as a duck-rabbit is a certain
kind of knowing one's way about. Certain gestures, for instance, which
indicate the duck- or the rabbit-aspect: fine shades of behavior.

But to gestures we can add other fine shades of behavior: language.
I might trace out the two long pointy things with my finger; I might
also accompany this gesture with words to the effect that I was indicating a duck's bill (and not a rabbit's ears). I would describe the
figure, in word and gesture, as a duck.

Let us now consider a more complex figure (henceforth to be called
the "Skull-Lady"), in the same family as the Duck-Rabbit, which can
be seen as a skull or a lady sitting at her vanity (frontispiece). To
indicate that I am seeing (say) the skull rather than the lady, I can,
just as in the case of the Duck-Rabbit, show that I know my way about
with a combination of gestures and remarks exhibiting the features of
the skull-aspect. The crucial difference is that in the case of the Duck-
Rabbit, the duck-features or rabbit-features, because of the extreme
simplicity of the figure, would be exhausted with two or three gestures, whereas the Skull-Lady presents an abundance of skull-fea-
tures or lady-features. Thus there is a sense in which you can pile
feature on feature to "convince" someone that you are seeing the skull-
aspect, much in the same way you can pile feature on feature to convince someone that Mr. A really is lazy or Mr. B really is intelligent.

And this brings us to a further point. Wittgenstein spoke of what tells
us that someone is seeing this aspect or that. But we can equally well
think of the procedure Wittgenstein outlines as a way of *defending*
one's aspect-ascription. Suppose I point to the Duck-Rabbit and say:
"It's a duck." And suppose that my statement is challenged. I could
support the aspect-ascription "It's a duck" much in the same way I
have been suggesting, following Wittgenstein, I show I am perceiving
the duck-aspect. With gestures and appropriate remarks I point out to
the person who raises the challenge what features can be seen as
features of a duck. The same method would be used to support the

[19] Wittgenstein, *Philosophical Investigations*, p. 203e.

aspect-ascription "It's a skull" or "It's a lady." But again with the crucial difference that my defense of the ascription "It's a duck" would be exhausted by revealing two or perhaps three duck-features, whereas my defense of the ascription "It's a skull" could enumerate feature on feature until one would be tempted to say that the defense is *overwhelming*; that no *normal* person could fail to see the skull-aspect; that a person who failed to see it under the impact of this marshalling of features was either aspect-blind or did not understand what was being said.

In another place I expressed the view that aspect-perceiving of the kind exemplified by the Duck-Rabbit seems to involve being able to pick out what I called there "crucial features."[20] I argued that it would seem very odd for someone to claim to see X as p – seeing the figure as a duck, for example – and be unable to mention any feature of X that could be construed as a feature of p. I am saying essentially the same thing here although with emphasis on the notion of *defending* one's aspect-ascription. It was objected to my earlier view, and might on the same grounds be objected to the present one, that there *are* cases in which it would not be odd to say X is p without being able to pick out any features of X that are p-like, cases where no defense of "X is p-like" can be expected to be forthcoming: cases where the claim to see X as p is "made at what Wittgenstein called the 'dawning' of an aspect," at a stage, in other words, where the aspect is not firmly perceived but is only just beginning to emerge in the perceiver's awareness.[21]

Now in a sense this criticism is a red herring; for although it begins with the justified suspicion that *all* aspect-ascriptions may not be defensible, it turns us from the direction in which genuine counter-examples might be found. *Of course* the awareness of what makes up a perception may come after the perception itself, as the working out of reasons why p is true may come *after* one has already grasped intuitively that p is true. Suppose I made the claim that a feature of theorems in Euclidean geometry is their (logical) demonstrability. It surely does not follow from this that it is never appropriate to assert p (a theorem in Euclidean geometry) and add "But I can't prove it." It goes without saying that one can come to suspect that p is true without being yet able to exhibit its proof. The proof comes after the insight,

---

[20] Peter Kivy, "Aesthetic Aspects and Aesthetic Qualities," *The Journal of Philosophy*, LXV (1968), pp. 89–93, *passim*.

[21] David Michael Levin, "More Aspects to the Concept of 'Aesthetic Aspects'," *The Journal of Philosophy*, LXV (1968), p. 485.

seldom along with or before it. And, likewise, I never intended in my discussion of "crucial features" to deny that there may be a stage in which one is vaguely aware of an aspect but cannot yet pick out its parts, nor do I want here to be understood to be denying that there may be a stage of aspect-awareness in which one cannot yet defend one's aspect-ascription.

The important question is not whether there is a stage in aspect-perceiving where crucial features cannot yet be picked out, where defense of an aspect-ascription cannot be produced, but whether there are cases of aspect-perceiving (of the Duck-Rabbit kind) in which there *never* comes a stage where the picking out of crucial features, the defense of the aspect-ascription, is possible. This, it seems to me, is the question which the foregoing criticism clouds. *If* there are such cases, then we will not be able to claim that *all* cases of aspect-ascribing even of the kind exemplified by the Duck-Rabbit are cases in which aspect-ascribing is condition-governed; for to be condition-governed is to be defensible, and being a defensible aspect-ascription requires crucial features to pick out. Let us examine such a possible case, suggested by Richard Wollheim's recent book *Art and Its Objects*.[22]

Imagine a dab of black paint on an otherwise blank canvas. It can be seen as a black dot either in front of or behind a white expanse; the figure will accommodate either perceptual interpretation. This seems to me a clear case of aspect-perceiving even more disarmingly simple than, yet in the same family as, the Duck-Rabbit.

Suppose now that Mr. A sees the figure as black in front of white and Mr. B sees it as black behind white. What crucial feature could Mr. A adduce to help Mr. B see the black-on-white aspect, to defend the black-on-white ascription? He could say: "The white can be seen as behind the black," or urge: "See the white as behind the black," or something of the kind. But to say "The white can be seen as behind the black," is to say nothing more than "The black can be seen as in front of the white," which is exactly the ascription to be defended; and to urge "See the white as behind the black," is hardly different than urging "See the black as in front of the white," which is exactly what Mr. B cannot see and what Mr. A is trying to help him to see. The figure is so simple that whichever aspect we grasp is grasped as a whole with no really distinguishable parts to constitute crucial features and provide the basis for a defense.

[22] Richard Wollheim, *Art and Its Objects: An Introduction to Aesthetics* (New York: Harper and Row, 1968), pp. 13–14.

The species of aspect-perceiving represented by Duck-Rabbit can be thought of as a series of figures of ascending complexity, from the absolute simplicity of the White-Canvas-with-Black-Spot to such intricate figures as the Skull-Lady, with Duck-Rabbit somewhere in the middle range. At some point along this series we pass from aspect-ascriptions that are not to aspect-ascriptions that are *defensible*. Where that line is to be drawn it is impossible to say exactly; but it is certainly clear that the White-Canvas-with-Black-Spot is on one side of it and the Skull-Lady on the other. Perhaps we might think of this series as one in which ascriptions are ranged from "X appears p to me" to "X is p." For in the former case no defense is called for; and in the latter case one is. Thus, to say that the canvas has a black-before-white aspect is to make a purely personal remark about how the figure appears to the one who makes the remark, whereas to say that the Skull-Lady has a skull-aspect is to go beyond the personal to an "objective" judgment for which a defense is called for and is possible. In short, to say "The canvas has a black-before-white aspect" is to make a statement of the "X seems p to me" kind, whereas to say "The Skull-Lady has a skull-aspect" is to make a statement of the "X is p" kind.

Now *if* aesthetic quality ascriptions were all aspect-ascriptions, and if all aspect-ascriptions were at the lower (less complex) end of our series, they would all be non-condition-governed. But there is no reason to believe that aesthetic aspect-ascriptions *would* be at the lower end. On the contrary, since aesthetic perception seems to be a complex rather than a simple affair, most (if not all) aesthetic aspect-ascriptions would be likely to be at the complex rather than the simple end of our scale. Perhaps the safest hypothesis, though, is that if all aesthetic perceiving were aspect-perceiving, aesthetic ascriptions would be a mixed bag of the simple, complex, and in between. And the safest conclusion, then, is that even if all aesthetic perceiving *were* aspect-perceiving, some – and perhaps most – aesthetic ascribing would still be condition-governed in the same sense as the ascription of the skull- or lady-aspect to the Skull-Lady is condition-governed.

In saying that the skull-ascription is condition-governed and (therefore) defensible whereas the black-before-white-ascription is neither, however, we are, as we have seen, saying that when we make the claim "It's a skull" we are making some kind of "objective" claim whereas when we make the claim "It's black-before-white" we are not. And to this it might be objected that seeing the skull- or lady-aspect of the Skull-Lady is a culturally conditioned phenomenon and, hence, not "objective" at all. A great deal of recent speculation has been highly critical of the notion that as drawings and paintings approach the status of the photograph, they approach some "objective" standard of realism; that whereas it might require an educated perception to recognize Rembrandt's drawing of an elephant as an elephant, the naive eye – the standard of objectivity – will always recognize a photograph of an elephant as an elephant. But that there is no naive eye has been persuasively (and I think conclusively) argued by E. H. Gombrich and Nelson Goodman. To quote the latter on the former,

as Ernest Gombrich insists, . . . there is no innocent eye. The eye comes always ancient to its work, obsessed by its own past and by old and new insinuations of the ear, nose, tongue, fingers, heart, and brain. It functions not as an instrument self-powered and alone, but as a dutiful member of a complex and capricious organism. Not only how but what it sees is regulated by need and prejudice. It selects, rejects, organizes, discriminates, associates, classifies, analyzes, constructs. It does not so much mirror as take and make. . . . [23]

To put the Skull-Lady on the objective end of a scale that rises from the subjective to the objective, then, might suggest that we are envisioning a scale with the Skull-Lady representing some kind of model of realism: that we are arguing that the skull-ascription is condition-governed, defensible, and (therefore) objective, ultimately, because the naive eye can always be depended upon to see the Skull-Lady as a skull. And if we are committed to this we surely fall afoul of Gombrich's and Goodman's annihilating criticism.

But we are committed to no such argument: we are not committed to saying that perception of the Skull-Lady cuts across cultural boundaries by virtue of some naive-eye doctrine of objectivity any more than we are committed to saying that the notions of "laziness" or "intelligence" cut across such boundaries. To be sure, an ancient Egyptian might not see the Skull-Lady as a skull or a lady at all; nor, however, might a Tahitian share our perceptions of laziness or a Buddhist our perceptions of intelligence. All we have ever claimed for the condition-governed model of aesthetic terms is that concept of "objectivity" which makes judgments of laziness or intelligence "objective" judgments; and that is all we need claim for the "objectivity" of aspect-ascriptions. That this "objectivity" is culturally conditioned, or that it is not the "objectivity" (say) of color perception, need cause us no undue concern. "Subjective" and "objective" are, of course, notoriously elusive notions (more of them later); and we have never gone beyond

[23] Nelson Goodman, *Languages of Art* (New York: Bobbs-Merrill, 1968), pp. 7–8.

the simple expedient of paradigm cases in defining them. These paradigms have committed us to nothing more than what the plain man
might be claiming if he were put in the position of having to insist
that "laziness" or "intelligence" are not simply "matters of taste."
In maintaining the "objectivity" of the skull- or lady-ascription, we
are claiming no more than this – least of all that the reality of the
Skull-Lady is guaranteed by the naive eye.

We must ask ourselves, finally, whether, even in the light of the above
analysis of the Skull-Lady, it makes sense to talk about *proving* the
frontispiece of this book is "A skull" or "A lady" or "A Skull-Lady."
Surely we can prove that Mr. A is intelligent or Mr. B is lazy (though
not, as we have seen, in the same way we can prove that 3 is a prime
number); and if the condition-governed model is to hold for aspect-
ascribing as well, it must make sense at least to talk about proving
that complex figures like Skull-Lady have skull- or lady-aspects. But
there are those who find it difficult to accept the notions of "proof"
and "evidence" in these contexts. Thus Tilghman, for example:

It can be proved to someone that a creature is a duck by pointing out the presence
of the characteristic duck-making features. While there are such "duck-making"
features whose presence, all things being equal, virtually force one to identify
the thing as a duck, there are no such features whose presence force me to see
the duck-rabbit picture as a duck.[24]

Tilghman's difficulty here – and it is not an isolated case – devolves,
I think, on the conflation of such phrases as "prove that...," "prove
to someone that...," and "get someone to see...." For the presence
of as many duck-making features as you like will *not* guarantee Mr. A
can prove *to Mr. B* (or anyone else) that an object before him is a (real)
duck: what it guarantees is that the object *is* a real duck, and that
there is a proof that it is. Likewise, the abundance of skull-making
features in the Skull-Lady guarantees that it is a skull; whether Mr. B
will see it is another question. To prove X is p to someone is to convince
someone that X is p; but to prove X is p is not necessarily to convince –
to prove to – *anyone* that X is p, is not necessarily to get anyone to see
that X is p, to see that Donald is a duck or the Skull-Lady a skull.
Further, to "get someone to see" Donald is a duck or the Skull-Lady a
skull one need not prove to him that Donald is a duck or the Skull-
Lady a skull. (One cannot, of course, prove to someone that Donald is a

[24] B. R. Tilghman, *The Expression of Emotion in the Visual Arts: A Philosophical Inquiry*
(The Hague: Martinus Nijhoff, 1970), pp. 77–78.

duck or the Skull-Lady a skull without at the same time getting them to see Donald as a duck or the Skull-Lady as a skull.) But even though one can get someone to see Donald is (or as) a duck without proving to him that Donald is a duck, we surely would not want to say that we cannot prove that Donald is a duck, or that there is no proof that Donald is a duck, or that the notion of "proof" is out of place here. And, similarly, even though one can get someone to see the Skull-Lady is (or as) a skull without proving to him that the Skull-Lady is a skull, there is no reason for us to say that we cannot prove the Skull-Lady is a skull, or that there is no proof that the Skull-Lady is a skull, or that the notion of "proof" is out of place here.

If we keep the three phrases "prove that...," "prove to someone that...," and "get someone to see..." distinct in our minds, we will see that it is a nonsequitur to say: (a) there are no features whose presence force me to see the Duck-Rabbit as a duck; therefore (b) there is no proof that the Duck-Rabbit is a duck. There is no proof that *Wittgenstein's* Duck-Rabbit is a duck – because of the paucity of duck-making features. But if Duck-Rabbit were made as complex as Skull-Lady, there *would* be a proof. Nevertheless, it would still be true that there are no features whose presence force me to see the Duck-Rabbit as a duck. To think that (b) follows from (a) is to confuse "proving that..." with "getting someone (namely me) to see..." or "proving to someone (namely me) that...."

If, then, we compare (say) "Mr. A is lazy" with "The frontispiece is a Skull-Lady," we will find that their relations to the phrases "prove that...," "prove to someone that...," and "get someone to see..." are pretty much alike. (1) I can prove – there is a proof – that Mr. A is lazy; and I can prove – there is a proof – that the frontispiece is a Skull-Lady. (2) No number of lazy-making features guarantees I can prove to Mr. B that Mr. A is lazy; and no number of skull-making or lady-making features guarantees I can prove to Mr. B that the frontis-piece is a Skull-Lady. (3) No number of lazy-making features guarantees my being able to get Mr. B to see that Mr. A is lazy; and no number of skull-making or lady-making features guarantees my being able to get Mr. B to see the frontispiece as a Skull-Lady. (4) I can get someone to see that Mr. A is lazy without necessarily proving to him that Mr. A is lazy; and I can get someone to see the frontispiece as a Skull-Lady without necessarily proving to him that it is a Skull-Lady. (5) If I prove to someone that Mr. A is lazy, I will, at the same time, have gotten him to see that Mr. A is lazy; and if I prove to someone that the frontispiece is a Skull-Lady, I will, at the same time, have gotten him to see it as a skull and as a lady. Thus, "prove that...," "prove to someone that...," and "get someone to see..." function alike among such condition-governed terms as "lazy" and such complex figures as the Skull-Lady, and are, therefore, as at home with the latter as with the former. The concept of "proof" is not incompatible with the concept of aspect-perceiving.

This much, then, is clear: there is a sense, closely parallel to the sense in which "lazy" and "intelligent" are condition-governed, in which aspect-ascriptions like "It's a skull" or "It's a lady" are condition-governed as well. There is the same notion of "piling up" evidence beyond which the ascriptions "lazy," "intelligent," "skull," "lady," cannot be denied without suggesting some anomaly on the part of the person who remains unperceiving. I do not wish to deny that there are great perplexities in the notion of aspect-perceiving which cry out for philosophical explication. Nor do I wish to minimize or slur over the differences between the logic of calling a man "intelligent" or "lazy" and calling the Skull-Lady "a skull" or "a lady." Nevertheless, there is this common ground: the possibility of piling up evidence to some kind of logically compelling conclusion; in short, condition-governed behavior. And this is the conclusion which we are seeking. It assures us that even if all aesthetic perceiving is aspect-perceiving and, by consequence, all aesthetic ascribing is aspect-ascribing, there is no reason to conclude that all aesthetic ascribing is non-condition-governed.

Recapitulation

In the opening section of this chapter we outlined some of the reasons why aspect-perceiving has seemed a potentially fruitful concept for aesthetics in general and, in particular, for those who accept the notion that aesthetic terms are not condition-governed. And we derived from the concept of aspect-perceiving an argument which tended to support the non-condition-governed behavior of aesthetic terms. This argument was: (1) aesthetic perceiving is aspect-perceiving; (2) therefore, aesthetic ascribing is aspect-ascribing; (3) aspect-ascribing is non-condition-governed; (4) therefore aesthetic ascribing is non-condition-governed or, in other words, aesthetic terms are non-condition-governed.

In the second section we dealt with the first premise of this argument, attempting to cast doubt on the contention that aesthetic perception is aspect-perception. We turned our attention, in the third section, to the third premise, and tried to show that aspect-ascribing of a certain kind, namely, ascribing exemplified by the Duck-Rabbit, is indeed condition-governed, at least in its more complex manifestations.

We have, at this juncture, both presented our condition-governed model of aesthetic terms and defended it against some major objections that have been or might be raised against it. Our argument has now run its course. It remains for us to make our conclusion.

CHAPTER VI

ART AND OBJECTIVITY

Two Footnotes to Plato

This book has been, to a large degree, polemical. It has presented a thesis, but has occupied itself more, perhaps, with defense than with exposition. There is some justification for this besides the disputative disposition of its author.

I believe G. E. Moore once said that a philosophical problem would never have occurred to him if he had not read philosophy books. And H. A. Wolfson expressed the view that all philosophy has been born of philosophy, except for the "first" philosopher, and, as Wolfson puts it, all Thales could see was water. The condition-governed model of aesthetic terms would not have stood in need of defense, or perhaps even of explication, if it had not been the subject of philosophical reflections. For why should one bother to defend, or take the trouble to present as a revelation what is, after all, quite innocent and common-place. Western man has been describing his art-works for a very long time, as long, perhaps, as he has been making them; and if we look to Homer for our first great literature, we can look there also for our first descriptions of works of art. What is there on a surface as yet untroubled by philosophy to make us think that these describings have been in any way "odd," "deceptive," "not really descriptions at all," "not really governed by conditions," in short, not like our endless descriptions of what ever else has interested us enough and seemed important enough to elicit them?

What I am driving at, here, is that to the theoretically non-committed observer, there is nothing particularly striking in the business of aesthetic discussion to suggest an absence of governing rules and conditions: nothing like the gnawing frustration of moral dilemmas or the devastating befuddlement of Zeno's paradoxes to drive us into the arms of epistemology and metaphysics – and, perhaps, scepticism. Reflecting on art would never have led me to doubt that aesthetic terms are condition-governed; reflecting on the reflections has – which is why the thesis that aesthetic terms *are* condition-governed has been put, for the most part, in the form of counter-reflections. Thus, in a way, I am presenting myself as a defender of aesthetic common sense. But one man's common sense may be another man's paradox, witness the fact that Berkeley and G. E. Moore were *both* defending it; and with friends like that common sense would scarcely need any enemies. So I will not ask the reader to accept *my* views as common sense and Sibley's (say) as paradoxical, but, rather, to accept my way of presenting my views, with my own particular taste in common sense as an apology for having so presented them.

It is not, then, to the "surface" of aesthetic phenomena that we can look for prima facie signs – even misleading ones – of the non-condition-governed behavior of aesthetic terms. And many of the arguments which have purported to demonstrate it we have already examined in detail. But our major themes have deep philosophical roots. If the non-condition-governed model of aesthetic terms is not "common sense," it has conceptual connections with philosophical traditions of such long standing that they have begun to seem like common sense to many of us.

If I were to choose one rubric under which to place the major arguments examined in this book I would choose the title "Art and the Irrational": that, it seems to me, is the theme that Sibley *et al.* are still working out. Perhaps the connections are remote – certainly they are remote in time from Plato's seminal statement – but for me the *Ion* and *Republic* are never out of mind when I am reading arguments to the effect that aesthetic terms are non-condition-governed and descriptive of the apparent but not the real. Let me pursue these connections for a moment.

We discussed, early on, the concept of "taste," and we asked what influence this concept might have in the direction of the conclusion that aesthetic terms are ungovernable. And how closely the concept of taste has been associated with the irrational tradition in art, even in its Platonic form, is not difficult to demonstrate.

In Plato's *Ion*, Socrates is seen cross-questioning a man whose profession is that of "rhapsode." Socrates describes the rhapsodes as "interpreters" of the poets;[1] and the rhapsode Ion (after whom the

---

[1] Plato, *Ion*, trans. W. R. M. Lamb, 535.

dialogue is called) is described as *a reciter* of Homer's poetry, *a commentator* on it, and *one who praises* it. And in each of these activities he, like the poet himself, is not governed by the rules of art but by "inspiration," by a divine madness. Thus, Ion the "performer": "when you give a good recitation and specially thrill your audience ... are you then in your senses, or are you carried out of yourself and does your soul in ecstasy suppose herself to be among the scenes you are describing...?"[2] Ion the "interpretive critic": "this is not an art in you, whereby you speak well on Homer, but a divine power. ..."[3] And, finally, Ion the "evaluative critic": "And when you ask me the reason why you can speak at large on Homer but not the rest [of the poets], I tell you it is because your skill in praising Homer comes not by art, but by divine dispensation."[4]

Ion has been cited since time out of mind as perhaps the primary source of the doctrine that in artistic *creation*, there is madness in the method: in other words, the urtext for "Art and the Irrational." But what is not often emphasized enough by commentators on the text is that Plato is not only talking here about the creator – as a matter of fact, *he* seems rather a side issue. It is the "critic" – if we may take the liberty of referring to the Greek rhapsode in this way – who is Socrates' subject of inquiry.[5] And he is compared to the poet in that just as the poet creates without knowing how he does it, without being governed by rules or method, so too does the critic analyze and judge the poem: "for it is not by art or knowledge about Homer that you say what you say, but by divine dispensation and possession...."[6]

It is not by chance that in the period which saw the rapid growth of the concept of "taste" in criticism, there were frequent references, and an obvious indebtedness to the Platonic theory of the artist "possessed," which has provided an ever-present authority for the innateness of aesthetic creativity. From its very beginnings in the sixteenth

---

[2] *Ibid.*

[3] *Ibid.*, 533.

[4] *Ibid.*, 536.

[5] For a defense of the *Ion* as an examination of criticism, see Craig La Drière, "The Problem of Plato's *Ion*," *Journal of Aesthetics and Art Criticism*, X (1951).

[6] *Ion*, 536. It is important to observe that Plato is concerned here only with the way we talk about *poetry*. In fact, he contrasts poetry-talk sharply with the way we talk about painting, sculpture, and music (532–533). One who knows painting, sculpture, or music can make knowledgeable judgments about *all* painting, sculpture, or music. But Ion can only say sensible things about *one* poet: Homer. And this is supposed to show, according to Socrates, that talking well about painting, sculpture, and music gives evidence of *knowledge*, whereas speaking well only of Homer does not give evidence of knowledge at all – hence the "inspiration" theory of the rhapsode. But as the modern system of the arts developed, Socrates' conclusion about poetry was extended to all of the other "fine arts" as well.

century, British criticism was imbued with this theory, yet in a naturalistic version that had been, for the most part, cleansed of its mysti-
cal connotations. George Puttenham wrote in *The Arte of English
Poesie* (1589) both of a "diuine instinct" and an "excellencie of nature"
which, he added, "the Platonicks call ... *furor*...."[7] Previously,
Philip Sidney, in the influential *An Apologie for Poetrie* (c. 1583), seems
to have rejected the mystico-religious notions of inspiration for a more
naturalistic notion of innate talent.

For Poesie must not be drawne by the eares; it must be gently led, or rather it
must lead. Which was partly the cause that made the auncient-learned affirme
it was a diuine gift, and no humaine skill. ... A poet no industrie can make, if
his own *Genius* bee not carried vnto it: and therefore is it an old Prouerbe,
Orator fit, Poeta nascitur.[8]

And early in the seventeenth century Francis Bacon expressed similar
views of natural endowment in art – specifically painting and music –
without a trace of mysticism (as one would expect in Bacon's case).
For Bacon, beauty is created "by a kind of felicity ... and not by
rule...."[9]

The notion of poetic genius as an innate – therefore in some sense an
"irrational" – faculty, which the Elizabethans connected with what
Puttenham called "Platonick *furor*," was supplemented in the seventeenth century by the addition of a psychological "location," the
imagination (fancy, or wit) which continued to exhibit the irrational
aspect of the inspiration theory. At the outset of the seventeenth
century, Bacon, in the *Advancement of Learning* (1605), set the stage
for this kind of thing with a three-fold division of human mental
faculties (not by any means original with him) in which "Poesie" was
assigned to the imagination. "THE PARTS of humane learning have
reference to the three partes of Mans vnderstanding, which is the seate
of Learning: HISTORY to his MEMORY, POESIE to his IMAGI-
NATION, and PHILOSOPHIE to his REASON." Imagination is the
lawless faculty of mind "which, being not tyed to the Laws of Matter,
may at pleasure ioyne that which Nature hath seuered, & seuer that
which Nature hath ioyned, and so make vnlawfull Matches & diuorses
of things...."[10] The imagination is "lawless" for Bacon, then, in that

[7] *Elizabethan Critical Essays*, ed. G. Gregory Smith (London: Oxford University Press,
1904), vol. II, p. 3.
[8] *Ibid.*, vol. I, p. 195.
[9] "Of Beauty," *Essays, Advancement of Learning, New Atlantis, and Other Pieces*, ed. R. F.
Jones (New York: Odyssey Press, 1937), p. 125.
[10] *Critical Essays of the Seventeenth Century*, ed. J. E. Spingarn (London: Oxford University Press, 1957), vol. I, pp. 4–5.

it is not subservient, in its creations, to the laws of nature or the physical constitution of the world – hence the "fiction" in poetry. Such notions were repeated throughout the seventeenth century with numerous variations and embellishments, two of the more notable contributors being Hobbes and Dryden.

What distinguishes the aesthetic psychology of the Elizabethan and seventeenth-century British critics from that represented by enlightenment concepts of "taste," is that, in the main, the former is a psychology of the *creator*, the latter a psychology of the *perceiver* – the critic and the audience. But the fact is that the line between creator and perceiver was not by any means so clearly drawn at the time. And just as in the *Ion*, the theory of inspiration and poetic madness served both for the poet and his interpreter, the rhapsode, so the imagination served in the seventeenth century as the faculty of perception as well as creation. So when Joseph Addison came to write the first extended examination in Britain of aesthetic *perception* (in 1712) he chose as the title "Pleasures of the Imagination." There was no hesitation on his part in choosing what had traditionally been the poet's *creative* faculty for the perceiver's *receptive* faculty. Such concepts as "imagination" and the like apparently performed a double service in the seventeenth century, having reference both to the creator and the perceiver. It is this circumstance which makes an unbroken connection between "taste" and the Platonic doctrine of art as irrational.

Thus the concept of taste is deeply imbedded in a philosophical tradition that makes of the critic as well as the creator a non-knower: one who does what he does in a kind of blind instinctual way, ungoverned by methods and rules, using "no art at all." It is not surprising, then, that those who have identified taste-terms with aesthetic terms have, for whatever other reasons, felt drawn to the conclusion that aesthetic terms are non-condition-governed, and those applying them somehow performing a slight-of-hand which reason, even in its informal contexts, knows nothing of. Platonism has impelled taste in that direction; and Sibley, I suggest, is a footnote to Plato.

But taste and the non-condition-governed behavior of aesthetic terms is only one of our principal themes: its persistent counterpoint is the doctrine of "aesthetic vision" which proclaims that aesthetic terms describe appearance and not reality. And this is the other side of the Platonic coin: specifically, Book X of the *Republic*, where we learn that the artist makes his bed but cannot sleep in it.

Plato's indictment of art and the artist in the *Republic* is a vexed subject which cannot possibly be taken up in detail here. All that I wish to do is indicate the most obvious line of thought relevant to the subject at hand, and that, of course, is the distinction between the real and the appearance, and the relation of the artist to it.

At the point near the end of the *Republic* where Socrates re-introduces the subject of art and the state (first undertaken in Books II and III), he has laid epistemological and metaphysical foundations – notably, the theory of forms – which are now made use of in a more rigorous examination of the artist's role than was heretofore possible. The Forms are injected into the discussion without much comment, as the dramatis personae (and the reader) can be assumed to be familiar with them already from previous conversations. So Socrates begins tersely: "Well then, shall we proceed as usual and begin by assuming the existence of a single essential nature or Form for every set of things which we call by the same name?"[11] He continues: "And we are in the habit of saying that the craftsman, when he makes the beds or tables we use or whatever it may be, has before his mind the Form of one or other of these pieces of furniture."

The artist, now, is contrasted with the maker of tables and beds:

take a mirror and turn it round in all directions. In a very short time you could produce sun and stars and earth and yourself and all the other animals and plants and lifeless objects which we mentioned just now.
Yes, in appearance, but not the actual things.
Quite so; you are helping out my argument. My notion is that a painter is a craftsman of that kind. You may say that the things he produces are not real; but there is a sense in which he too does produce a bed.
Yes, the appearance of one.[12]

But to produce the appearance of a bed is not to present the bed "as it is"; for that would not be a representation of the bed but a replica of it – another bed. Thus:

you may look at a bed or any other object from straight in front or slantwise or at any angle. Is there any difference in the bed itself, or does it merely look different?
It only looks different.
Well, that is the point. Does painting aim at reproducing any actual object as it is, or the appearance of it as it looks? In other words, is it a representation of the truth or of a semblance?
Of a semblance.
The art of representation, then, is a long way from reality.[13]

[11] *Republic*, trans. F. M. Cornford, 596.
[12] *Ibid.*, 597.
[13] *Ibid.*, 598.

Nor are the poets any closer to the real, for "all poetry from Homer onwards, consists in representing a semblance of its object, whatever it may be, including any kind of human excellence, with no real grasp of the reality."[14]

If we speak with the vulgar, we can represent Plato as maintaining that the poet and painter depict mere appearances of things, not the realities. And translating vulgar speech into slightly outmoded twentieth-century philosopher-talk, we can describe Plato as maintaining, with Tomas, that aesthetic vision is concerned with the appearance, not the stimulus object, although Tomas clearly is working with a perceptual distinction bequeathed to him by the eighteenth-century, not Plato's basically epistemological one. But if, of course, we speak with the learned, it is not quite so simple. For in the Academy, the Form of the bed is the "really real," the carpenter's bed but an appearance, and the poet's or painter's bed "at the third remove from reality." Nevertheless, the theme is there. And if taste and the non-condition-governed model of aesthetic terms is a footnote to Plato, its shadow, the dictum that aesthetic terms describe appearance only, is another. The themes we have been playing upon are as old as philosophy itself.

Aesthetic Terms and Aesthetic Qualities

What is the relationship between these two persistent themes that Plato introduced into our thinking about the arts? It is this: that they both concern, to use Nelson Goodman's fine phrase, "the way the world is" (or isn't). In the *Ion*, Socrates poses the question, Are the things we say about poetry *defensible*? Can Ion give *reasons* for saying this about Homer rather than the other? And the answer Plato gives is that the things we say about poetry are *not* defensible; that Ion *cannot* give reasons for saying this about Homer rather than that. When Ion does say his "fine things" about Homer's poetry, it is by divine dispensation; and, one wonders if this is not just a Platonic euphemism for blind luck. Are we not perilously close, too, to the view that Ion is not "possessed" by the god but merely by his own feelings towards the poetry about which he speaks? Is it any wonder, then, that the views on poetry expressed in the *Ion* should give birth to the views on art expressed in the *Republic*; that what we would call "aesthetic qualities" are sent into outer darkness, into the world of appearances,

[14] *Ibid.*, 600.

shadows, reflections, non-being? Let us not attribute to Plato a distinction between "subjective" and "objective" that belongs to a later age. But his views on art, in the hands of those who possess such a distinction, that way tend: towards the position that aesthetic remarks are not about the way the world is but about the way the observer is and the world appears to him.

But if we argue that aesthetic descriptions are *defensible*, we are committed to the view that aesthetic terms do name part of the world's furniture. And one common way of putting this is to say that aesthetic terms are the names of qualities, or, more emphatically, objective qualities. Certainly I seem to be committed to some such view as this in espousing the condition-governed model of aesthetic terms. Now, I suppose, I will have to pay the piper; for nothing has seemed more ephemeral and less real, more "subjective" and less "objective," to more philosophers, from Plato onwards, than aesthetic descriptions. "Let's get down to brass tacks" is such a common response of the "rational" man to an aesthetic remark that someone who is committed to the view that aesthetic remarks can be just as brass as anything else must surely put up some kind of defense. I represented myself, in the opening of this chapter, as the champion of aesthetic common sense. But here, to paraphrase Hume, is a species of philosophical common sense (if that is not too much of an oxymoron) that seems contradictory to my own.

Let me begin my defense with the question, Are aesthetic terms the names of qualities?

One thing, I think, is certain: aesthetic terms do not name *simple* qualities like redness or blueness. It is a plain fact of ordinary discourse that we can (and do) say things like: "X is p in virtue of its having this, that, or the other feature," where p is an aesthetic term. But we simply cannot (and do not) ever say in ordinary (non-technical) discourse: "X is red (or blue) in virtue of its having this, that, or the other feature." There is no feature besides redness that we can point to in an object in support of the assertion "It is red." If "red" is the name of a simple quality in virtue of this behavior, then aesthetic terms cannot be the names of simple qualities.

To the view that aesthetic terms name complex qualities, however, there seems to be a powerful rejoinder. It is obvious to some, at least, that we do not usually look at, listen to, or otherwise perceive a work of art in a calculating way when we are attending to it aesthetically. If I were looking at a prospective employee, I might size him up for intelligence (say) by mentally counting the intelligent-making features that he had and reaching the conclusion "Yes, he seems quite bright," or "No, he's pretty dull," as the case may be. But, it might be argued, when I am enjoying a painting or a piece of music I do not calculate in this way, counting up features towards reaching some conclusion, although I might certainly say, after a while, "Highly unified," or even right off, "My how delicate." And if I were asked what I had heard or seen, I might say: "Well it simply seems to have this delicate quality or this quality of unity." As a recent writer has put it, aesthetic features are "perceived as qualifying the object," and "To this extent, aesthetic ascriptions resemble descriptions of an object's color."[15] Unity and delicacy, unlike intelligence, seem like the redness of the apple.

Let us consider for a moment the phrase "perceived as qualifying the object." One major use of the "perceive as" locution is a contrary-to-fact use where we say "We perceive X as p" to indicate (1) that X really isn't p at all, and (2) that our experience of perceiving X is like the experience we would be having *if* X *were* p, or like the experience we have in perceiving things that are p. Thus, when Santayana said "Beauty is an emotional element, a pleasure of ours, which nevertheless we regard as a quality of things,"[16] I would take him to have been saying (1) that beauty is not a quality of things, and (2) that our experience of perceiving beauty is like our experience would have been if beauty were a quality of things, or is like our experience of perceiving p's that are qualities of things. Now if redness is our paradigm case of a quality of things, it seems that at least one of the conditions necessary for the use of the "perceive as" locution is fulfilled when we say that aesthetic predicates refer to features which we perceive as qualities of objects; for redness is a simple quality, and, as we have seen, aesthetic qualities cannot be. Hence, to say "We perceive the features that aesthetic terms name as *simple* qualities of objects" is correct in so far as aesthetic terms do not name simple qualities of objects. The negative, contrary-to-fact requirement is satisfied. But is the second requirement satisfied? Is our experience of perceiving the qualities named by aesthetic terms like our experience of perceiving simple qualities such as redness?

I confess that it is not altogether clear to me just how we would answer the question. But if I introspect – and I suppose my introspective reports are worth about as much or as little as anyone else's –

[15] Marcia Cavell, "Critical Dialogue," *The Journal of Philosophy*, LXVII (1970), p. 340.
[16] George Santayana, *The Sense of Beauty* (New York: Random House, 1955), p. 50.

then I can grant that *some* of the aesthetic features named by aesthetic terms *do* seem to be experienced in a way at least not unlike the way we experience redness; and, on the other hand, some seem to me to be experientially very different. Delicacy and garishness in paintings, for example, seem in my experience more like the redness of the apple than anything else. But unity in music, and vividness in prose, seem to me experientially very unlike seeing red apples or blue roses.

Our firm conclusion remains, then, that aesthetic terms do not name simple qualities; but we have reached, too, the rather weaker and vaguer conclusion that our experience in perceiving the qualities named by aesthetic terms perhaps may be, in some cases, very like our experience in perceiving simple qualities, although in some cases it may be very unlike. It is a vague conclusion because we are not at all clear just what exactly it means to say our experience in perceiving some aesthetic qualities is like (or unlike) our experience in perceiving simple qualities; and it is weak just because we are not clear about what it is we have concluded or how one would go about concluding it.

Having reached the conclusion, then, that aesthetic terms do not name simple qualities, we can now reach the further conclusion that either they do not name any qualities at all, or that they name complex qualities. Do they name any qualities at all? Or, to put that question in a more manageable form, do aesthetic terms obey the logic of (complex) quality-terms?

Well, if aesthetic terms name qualities – and from now on we will understand by "quality" "complex quality" – then there must be conditions or rules governing their application. If p names a quality, there must be some kind of procedure – "a certain routine," as Toulmin puts it[17] – for determining when it is appropriate to conclude "X is p." This is the logic of quality-terms; and it is, of course, the logic we tried to reveal in the behavior of aesthetic terms in the beginning of this book.

Again, if aesthetic terms name qualities, it must sometimes be appropriate to say "X seems p but really it isn't," "X is p but doesn't seem to be," and the like, where p is an aesthetic term; for this too is part and parcel of the logic of quality-terms. If p names a quality, it must make sense to say both "seems p" and "is p"; and we tried to show, earlier, that this requirement is indeed met by at least some aesthetic terms.

So, really, a major part of this book has been an extended argument

17 Toulmin, *op. cit.*, p. 10.

to the effect that some aesthetic terms do name qualities. And to ask, at this point, whether aesthetic terms name qualities at all is to ask a question that has already been answered. The answer is "Yes," and the reasons for that answer have already been given.

But we felt the thesis that aesthetic terms name qualities is in need of some further justification. What can that justification be? Perhaps if we locate the uneasiness that remains in entertaining this thesis we will be able to offer that further justification. And it seems to me that that uneasiness has something to do with the question, How much disagreement will we countenance in aesthetic matters? No one would think it appropriate to spend very much time convincing Jones that artichokes are really delicious when Jones thinks they are disgusting. There is, clearly, wide disagreement countenanced in our descriptions of the goodness and badness of foods. Whereas our attitude towards a disagreement about whether Jones is lazy or Smith intelligent would not so easily be dismissed with a shrug. Our attitude towards these is not one of complete tolerance: someone, we feel, must be right, and someone wrong. Now how wide are our disagreements in aesthetic descriptions? How lenient are our attitudes towards them? Are our disagreements and attitudes commensurate with the thesis that aesthetic terms name qualities? These are the questions we must explore in closing.

Aesthetic Terms and Aesthetic Disagreements

(1) What is our attitude towards disagreements in aesthetic descriptions? We are asking here not for the kind of survey of attitudes that a pollster might produce but, rather, some kind of linguistic intuition; some kind of firm feeling about what the appropriate response would be if someone delivered the judgment "X is p," where p is an aesthetic term, and the judgment was contradicted by someone else. If, for example, I were to say that dropping the atomic bomb on Hiroshima was the right thing to do, many would disagree; and their responses would not be likely to be the response of an artichoke hater to an artichoke lover. There would be arguments and counter-arguments: facts adduced and their ethical relevance questioned or denied; ethical principles enunciated and appealed to; ethical principles denounced and counter-principles invoked in their place. In short, our linguistic behavior in moral contexts would suggest strongly that questions of right and wrong are questions about which we can be

correct and incorrect; about which we can have genuine and not just apparent disagreements. This, I imagine, is the kind of linguistic argument behind G. E. Moore's statement that "It is surely plain matter of fact that when I assert an action to be wrong, and another man asserts it to be right, there sometimes is a real difference of opinion between us: he sometimes is denying the very thing which I am asserting."[18] We have, then, a firm feeling about the general character of moral discourse, and it is that moral discourse is, at least on the surface, compatible with moral theories which leave room for genuine moral disagreements and is incompatible with moral theories (such as *naive* emotivism) which do not allow for it.

What we are asking for, then, is a similar determination for aesthetic discourse to the one that has been made for moral discourse. And there is a long philosophical tradition, previously alluded to, which has attempted one. Let us see what its conclusions have been.

Hume represented critical disputes, as we have seen, as suspended between two equally attractive common sense notions: (1) that there is no disputing about tastes, and (2) that there are cases in which one man's critical judgment is clearly correct and another man's monstrous. Kant cast Hume's informal dilemma into a formal "antinomy of taste":

1. *Thesis.* The judgement of taste is not based upon concepts; for, if it were, it would be open to dispute (decision by means of proofs).
2. *Antithesis.* The judgement of taste is based on concepts; for otherwise, despite diversity of judgement, there could be no room even for contention in the matter (a claim to the necessary agreement of others with this judgement).[19]

But although Kant thus took over Hume's critical paradox, he did not seem to see it, as Hume had done, as a characterization of the plain man's attitude in ordinary aesthetic discourse. Hume saw critical discourse as composed of "mixed" linguistic commitments: two-faced in attitude. Kant, however, saw it as strongly committed to the "objective": the *antithesis*. Kant wrote (in section 7 of the third *Critique*):

As regards the *agreeable* every one concedes that his judgement, which he bases on a private feeling, and in which he declares that an object pleases him, is restricted merely to himself personally. Thus he does not take it amiss, if, when he says that Canary-wine is agreeable, another corrects the expression and reminds him that he ought to say: It is agreeable *to me*. ...
The beautiful stands on quite a different footing. It would, on the contrary, be ridiculous if any one who plumed himself on his taste were to think of justifying himself by saying: This object (the building we see, the dress that person

[18] G. E. Moore, *Ethics* (London: Oxford University Press, 1958), pp. 63–64.
[19] *Critique of Aesthetic Judgement*, p. 206.

has on, the concert we hear, the poem submitted to our criticism) is beautiful *for me*. For if it merely pleases *him*, he must not call it beautiful. ... but when he puts a thing on a pedestal and calls it beautiful, he demands the same delight from others. He judges not merely for himself, but for all men, and then speaks of beauty as if it were a property of things.[20]

Eighteenth-century philosophy, then, bequeathed to us two characterizations of aesthetic discourse: Hume's, the mixed view, which saw it as fallen between the subjective and objective stools; Kant's, the monistic view, which saw it as unequivocally objective in appearance.

Both views have had expression in contemporary philosophy. Harold Osborne, who has already been quoted on this regard, sees aesthetic discourse basically the way that Kant did: "In section 7 of the *Critique of Judgement* Kant was offering a reasonably accurate and penetrating phenomenological analysis [of aesthetic discourse] which must at least be taken into account by any [aesthetic] theory which does not accept it at face value."[21] But J. D. Mabbott, on the other hand, gravitates in a Humean direction. "In aesthetics," he writes,

... the situation seems to me to be fluid. Some ordinary men do use "beautiful" in accordance with subjectivist rules which make it equivalent to "I enjoy and approve." For example, they expect and are not at all worried by divergence and changes of taste. They do not condemn other people whose taste differs from theirs as poseurs or perverted or blind.

Yet, he continues,

I doubt whether any practising artist or critic will ever use aesthetic words according to subjectivist rules. It is the outsider, who "knows what he likes," who tends to be subjectivist.[22]

Which of these characterizations is the more accurate? It seems to me that the very existence of two conflicting views would lend some support at least to the Humean characterization of aesthetic discourse. For Hume, in the eighteenth century, and Mabbott, in the twentieth, are surely reporting their own linguistic attitudes; and I see no reason to think that their attitudes do not reflect some significant segment of aesthetic language-users. But the really important point for us to note is that whether the Kant-Osborne, or the Hume-Mabbott characterization is the more accurate, is *not* an important question for us because neither attempts to characterize the kind of aesthetic discourse

[20] *Ibid.*, pp. 51–52.
[21] "Wittgenstein On Aesthetics," p. 386.
[22] J. D. Mabbott, "Freewill and Punishment," *Contemporary British Philosophy*, Third Series, ed. H. D. Lewis (London: George Allen and Unwin; New York: Macmillan, 1961), pp. 306–07.

in which aesthetic terms predominate; both are concerned solely with evaluational aesthetic language: that is, statements that simply say "X is good," or "X is bad," or something synonymous. Further, I suspect, those who would argue that the condition-governed behavior of aesthetic terms is not consistent with the appearance of aesthetic discourse are guilty of an *ignoratio elenchi*; for the aesthetic discourse they are talking about, no matter what its character, invariably turns out to be discourse of the most unequivocally *evaluative* kind, in which aesthetic terms do not occur at all. Whenever someone says that our linguistic behavior in aesthetic matters is thus-and-so, the chances are that the aesthetic matters he has in mind are questions concerning the goodness and badness of works of art, perhaps because until quite recently these are the matters which have dominated aesthetic specu-lation, whereas the question, What is our attitude towards disagree-ments in aesthetic descriptions?, has scarcely been given serious consideration at all.

Do we, then, have any firm intuition about disputes (say) over whether X is unified, or Y is delicate, or Z is garish? In attempting to answer this question, one obvious pitfall should, at the outset, be pointed out and avoided. To say something is "a matter of taste" is, of course, to suggest that our attitude towards it is of a purely sub-jective kind. And since discussions of aesthetic terms usually begin by characterizing them as *taste*-terms, there is obviously going to be a tendency to think of the application of aesthetic terms as "a matter of taste," thus suggesting that our attitude towards "X is p," where p is an aesthetic term, is an attitude of complete subjective indifference. However, we should by now be sufficiently aware of the *two* concepts of taste distinguished in Chapter II to see immediately that this is a completely unjustified move. For the "taste" which is necessary for the application of aesthetic terms – the ability to notice or see or tell that things have certain qualities – is *not* the "taste" about which there is no disputing, and is not, in ordinary discourse, "taste" at all. The fact that aesthetic terms are taste-terms in a special, coined sense of "taste" in no way suggests that our attitude towards the application of aesthetic terms is the attitude which the "normal" sense of "taste" bestows, namely, "each to his own taste."

That aesthetic terms, many of them, at least, are taste-terms, then, does not indicate that the realm of discourse they occupy is subjective in character. But our original question remains to be answered: Is the appearance of descriptive aesthetic discourse "subjective," "objective," or, perhaps, "mixed"? It appears to me that there is no reason to think it subjective. There does not seem to be an attitude of easy acceptance, complete tolerance, with regard to judgments of the kind "X is p," where p is an aesthetic term. The largest concession to subjectivism that we can make is to characterize descriptive aesthetic disputes as mixed.

If Mr. A says that the *Eroica* is unified, and Mr. B says that it is disorganized, Mr. A is not going to react in the same way to Mr. B's assertion as he would if he were disagreeing with Mr. B over whether an artichoke is nasty or nice. Reasons and arguments are surely going to be forthcoming. But suppose, now, that Mr. A defends his assertion that the *Eroica* is unified by pointing out the monothematic structure of the movements; and suppose Mr. B acknowledges the presence of the monothematic structure but still insists that it is not unified. *Now* Mr. A might take an attitude of easy acquiescence; and *in so doing* he might perhaps be acknowledging that the dispute has *become* valuational. This will be so, of course, only if Mr. A's attitude towards aesthetic valuations is a subjective one; and since evaluative aesthetic discourse seems to be mixed, the subjective attitude will not always be the one taken when a dispute over the application of an aesthetic term becomes a valuational dispute.

Our conclusion then is this: the appearance of disagreements over the application of aesthetic terms in aesthetic descriptions is basically Kantian, that is, objective; the appearance of disagreements in aesthetic value is Humean, that is, mixed. And the change from the objective to the subjective, which may occur in a dispute over the application of some particular aesthetic term, may indicate that the dispute has been acknowledged, either explicitly or implicitly, to have become a valuational one. There is no reason to believe that our attitude towards such questions as "Is X unified?," "Is Y delicate?," "Is Z garish?," is, then, any different from our attitude towards such questions as "Is Mr. A intelligent?," or "Is Mr. B lazy?," which is an attitude basically expecting there to be a correct and an incorrect answer. And that our attitude to these questions sometimes changes at some crucial point is a sign of some basic change in the question, although not in the words in which the question is asked.

(2) How wide are our disagreements in aesthetic descriptions? The question is an important one for us because, as Sibley says, "where unresolved disputes are endemic and widespread (as they are said to be

in the aesthetic realm), matters are not objective."[23] Nevertheless, it must be borne in mind that endemic and widespread disputes about p's is not a sufficient condition for p's being non-objective; nor is widespread agreement a sufficient condition for p's being objective. For we might, as a matter of fact, be so constituted that we could not ever reach any significant agreement about p's and yet p's might be objective for all of that; and, on the other hand, we might all be so constituted as to be in universal agreement about the niceness of artichokes, yet "Artichokes are nice" might still be a subjective judgment. Thus we can only take widespread and endemic disputes in aesthetic descriptions as a disturbing warning that aesthetic descriptions *may* not be objective; and, conversely, we can take widespread agreement only as an encouraging sign that they might be objective. The question is by no means clinched either way regardless of what we conclude about the extent of disagreement in aesthetic descriptions.

Matters are further complicated by the fact that when people discuss aesthetic disagreements, they can almost always be counted upon, as we have seen, to mean aesthetic diasgreements about goodness and badness of aesthetic objects, not disagreements about the appropriateness of aesthetic terms. Thus, much of the previous work already done to determine the extent of aesthetic agreement or disagreement, whatever its merits, is work that is quite irrelevant to the present question. Even, then, if Hume (for example) were correct in urging that "This variety of taste is obvious to the most careless inquirer, so will it be found, on examination, to be still greater in reality than in appearance,"[24] we must dismiss the conclusion as not to the purpose; for Hume is talking about the magnitude of conflicting critical value judgments, and the variety of aesthetic likes and dislikes, not about conflicting judgments as to whether works of art are unified or delicate or garish.

Nor are we out of the woods if we simply resolve to exclude from consideration disagreements of the more obviously evaluative kind. For, as we have had occasion to observe before, some disputes about the appropriateness of aesthetic descriptions are, in fact, thinly disguised evaluative disputes. Thus, "what we might regard as exclusively aesthetic terms almost invariably do have evaluative force, so that a dispute as to whether a Tintoretto is garish or vivid may in-

[23] Sibley and Tanner ,"Objectivity and Aesthetics," p. 34.
[24] "Of the Standard of Taste," p. 3.

volve a difference of aesthetic perception or a difference of [aesthetic value] judgment."[25] In other words, a dispute in aesthetic terms may turn out, on scrutiny, to be an evaluative dispute. And an evaluative dispute does not count as evidence of the prevalence of disputes about aesthetic terms, even if it is a dispute in which the application of aesthetic terms is at stake.

But even if we are sure to exclude from consideration disputes about aesthetic evaluation, both of the obvious and of the disguised kind, we are not by any means prepared to meet head on the task of estimating the prevalence of unresolvable disputes in aesthetic description. We face a similar problem here that the ethical theorist faces in determining the prevalence of unresolvable ethical disputes; and perhaps it would be instructive to examine briefly what the ethical problem is.

Suppose that Mr. A and Mr. B disagree about whether Mr. C was right or wrong in killing his wife.[26] But suppose further that Mr. A believes Mrs. C was suffering from an excruciatingly painful, lingering, and always fatal disease, and that Mr. B believes she was in perfect health and had a very large life insurance policy naming her husband as sole beneficiary. Mr. A, then, sees the killing of Mrs. C as a commendable (or at least defensible) act of mercy, whereas Mr. B sees it as a ruthless and unjustifiable killing for personal gain. They are not really disagreeing about the rightness or wrongness of the same act; and both might agree that mercy killings are morally justifiable and killings for personal gain are morally unjustifiable. Thus their dispute would disappear if they came to agree on the facts of the case; and they do not differ over an "ultimate ethical principle,"[27] since both probably agree about the relevant ethical principles, "Mercy killing is morally justifiable," and "Killing for personal gain is morally unjustifiable." Hence the prevalence of disputes like the one Mr. A and Mr. B are having does not constitute the kind of evidence that would (say) lend support to ethical relativism.

Similarly, not every dispute about whether X is p or not-p, where p is an aesthetic term, is going to be evidence for the assertion that the condition-governed model of aesthetic terms is incompatible with the prevalence of disagreements about aesthetic descriptions. Some disagreements are going to be judged irrelevant here, just as some ethical

---

[25] Sibley and Tanner, *op. cit.*, p. 66. The remark quoted is Tanner's.
[26] Cf. R. B. Brandt, *Ethical Theory* (Englewood Cliffs, N.J.: Prentice-Hall, 1959) pp. 99–101.
[27] *Ibid.*

disagreements must be judged irrelevant to the question of ethical relativism. What is our criterion for relevance?

If Mr. A said "X is p," and Mr. B said "X is not -p,"where p is an aesthetic term, we would certainly want to be sure that both Mr. A and Mr. B were talking about the same object when they said "X." This appears a trivial enough demand; but, after all, Mr. A and Mr. B seemed to be talking about the same action when they were disagreeing about the rightness or wrongness of Mr. C's killing his wife, and it turned out upon investigation that they were not. And when one realizes the complexity of many works of art, and the likelihood that one or both of the parties to a dispute over whether X is p or not might be missing some important p- or not-p-making feature of X, the requirement is not so trivial as it first might seem to be. If Mr. A takes X to have nonaesthetic properties, x, y, and z, and Mr. B does not, and if x, y, and z are p-making features, we would surely not want to say that the disagreement over whether X is p lends support to the contention that p is not really a quality at all. Our requirement, then, for a dispute being relevant to the question of aesthetic objectivity is that the parties agree about what nonaesthetic properties the aesthetic object possesses, and that *all* relevant nonaesthetic features – that is, all p- or not-p-making features, where the dispute is over X being p or not-p – are being perceived.

Consider, for example, the long-standing dispute over the objectivity of expressive qualities in music. If the music is really sad in some objective sense, if sadness is a quality of the music, surely, it has been argued, we would expect some kind of general consensus as to what emotive qualities a given musical segment possesses. Yet, as Eduard Hanslick long ago urged, against the devotees of emotion in music,

Let them play the theme of a symphony by Mozart or Haydn, an adagio by Beethoven, a scherzo by Mendelssohn, one of Schumann's or Chopin's compositions for the piano, anything, in short, from the stock of our standard music; or again, the most popular themes from overtures by Auber, Donizetti, and Flotow. Who would be bold enough to point out a definite feeling as the subject of any of these themes? One will say "love." He may be right. Another thinks it is "longing." Perhaps so. A third feels it to be "religious fervor." Who can contradict him?[28]

And in a similar vein, Edmund Gurney wrote, "the great 'subject' of the first movement of Schubert's B flat trio, ... represents to me and many others the *ne plus ultra* of energy and passion; yet this very movement was described by Schumann as 'tender, girlish, confiding':

[28] Eduard Hanslick, *The Beautiful in Music*, trans. Gustav Cohen (New York: Liberal Arts Press, 1957), p. 29.

and the reiteration of the bass figure in the adagio of Beethoven's fourth symphony, which has always seemed to me quite tremendous in its earnestness, appeared to Schumann as a humorous feature."[29]

Now, clearly, not every dispute over the emotive qualities of a piece of music can count as a relevant dispute. We must ask ourselves, Have the two disputants perceived the same nonaesthetic features, specifically, the same emotion-making features, where the dispute is about whether a theme or a movement has or has not some specific emotive quality? Have they perceived the same object? Charles Hartshorne writes, "The assumption that persons whose sense of the [emotive] meaning of a piece of music differs can yet have the very same sense perception of the sounds is, so far as I know, devoid of all evidence."[30] And Vincent Tomas, after the same quarry, argues:

Suppose that when two subjects listen to an orchestra playing a tune with a brisk tempo, one of them reported that the music he heard was solemn, and the other reported that the music he heard was gay. How shall we interpret this fact? Possibly the subjects heard "the same music," but each experienced a different feeling import. But possibly the difference in feeling import is due to the fact that they did not hear "the same music." To decide between these possibilities we need first to apply some criterion which tells us when the music two people hear is "the same." I have no idea what that criterion might be.[31]

What Hartshorne and Tomas seem to want to say, then, is that there may really be *no* genuine disputes about the specific emotive content of any piece of music: all disputes may be seeming ones only, because when Mr. A says that X is solemn, and Mr. B says that it is gay, Mr. A may really be talking about a different object than Mr. B, although they are both misleadingly calling it by the same name. Taking a leaf from their book, we might argue that there may be no genuine disputes about *any* aesthetic terms: that whenever Mr. A and Mr. B seem to disagree about whether X is p or not-p (where p is an aesthetic term), one or both are either failing to perceive nonaesthetic p- (or not-p-) making features possessed by X or are taking X to possess nonaesthetic p- (or not-p-) making features which in fact it does not possess. And there is no way I can see of dislodging anyone from this position; for no one can ever say with certainty that we are aware of all the relevant nonaesthetic features in any given instance.

[29] Edmund Gurney, *The Power of Sound* (London: Smith, Elder, and Co., 1880), pp. 339–40.
[30] Charles Hartshorne, *Philosophy and Psychology of Sensation* (Chicago: University of Chicago Press, 1934), p. 186.
[31] "The Concept of Expression in Art," pp. 42–43.

But it appears to me too easy a way to take with disagreements about aesthetic terms simply to claim that all such disagreements arise out of some misapprehension of the nonaesthetic facts, although, as I have said, I know no way of refuting someone who was to take this heroic line, except to note that it savors of essentially *legislating* all disagreement out of existence; for if we say that there is genuine disagreement if and only if p and not-p are predicated of the "same object," and if we then say that a necessary condition for being the "same object" is that p and not-p not be predicated of it, then no genuine disagreement can ever exist – *by stipulative definition*. However we can certainly conclude that many – if not all – aesthetic disputes over the applicability of aesthetic terms may be caused by a failure to perceive present nonaesthetic features or by the "perception" of nonaesthetic features that are absent. And the only disagreements relevant to the question are those which persist even when the perception of all nonaesthetic features is completely accurate. The number of relevant disputes over aesthetic terms, then, may be considerably less than the number of disputes in which one party says "X is p," and another party "X is not-p" (where p is an aesthetic term).

How many such relevant disputes are there? And is that number larger than would be expected on the hypothesis that aesthetic terms name qualities? Our answers to both of these questions must be disappointing. For the plain facts are that no one really knows the extent of aesthetic disagreement concerning aesthetic terms. And if they did, it would be no help at all in determining whether the objectivity of aesthetic terms is compatible with this number because no one seems to know either how much disagreement would be *too much* or how little agreement would be *too little*.[32] In a symposium on "Objectivity and Aesthetics," from which we have already quoted, Sibley raises the rhetorical question, "are we sure that sceptics do not vastly exaggerate the amount of unresolved disagreement about aesthetic descriptions that exists, perhaps by looking too narrowly or being blind to the obvious?,"[33] clearly expecting "No" for an answer; while his co-symposiast, Michael Tanner, believes "that Sibley is unduly optimistic about the facts, or even the real possibilities, of aesthetic agreement."[34] But all we can say with any certainty, I think, is that there is as yet absolutely no reason to believe the extent of disagreements over

[32] Sibley and Tanner, *op. cit.*, p. 38.
[33] *Ibid.*, p. 35.
[34] *Ibid.*, p. 63   .

aesthetic terms too great to accommodate the hypothesis of their objectivity. The evidence is simply inconclusive either way.

Conclusion

In this, the concluding chapter, I have represented the general thesis defended in the preceding chapters, namely, that aesthetic terms are condition-governed, as a species of common sense which, however, has been subverted by a long tradition of philosophical speculation reaching as far back as Plato's seminal reflections on poetry, painting, and music. This comes to focus, I argued, in the question of aesthetic objectivity, that is to say, the question, Do aesthetic terms name objective qualities of the world?

The answer forthcoming was, first, that aesthetic terms do not name simple qualities (like redness or blueness), since the assertion "X is p," where p is an aesthetic term, can be defended by further assertions about the properties of X, whereas the assertion "X is red (or blue)" cannot. The conclusion was, then, that either aesthetic terms name complex qualities or they name no qualities at all.

It had been the general argument of the previous chapters that aesthetic terms *do* exhibit the logic of complex quality terms (like "lazy" and "intelligent"). Nevertheless, two nagging questions yet remained: (1) Are our attitudes towards aesthetic disagreements compatible with the hypothesis that aesthetic terms name qualities? (2) Is the number of the seemingly unresolvable disagreements in aesthetic descriptions larger than would be expected on the hypothesis that aesthetic terms name qualities?

Our answer to the first question was that there seems to be no incompatibility of our attitudes towards aesthetic disagreements with the condition-governed model and the objectivity which it implies. And our answer to the second question was that once irrelevant aesthetic disagreements are disregarded – and these include aesthetic value disagreements and aesthetic disagreements in which the parties are not clear as to the nonaesthetic facts of the case – the number of aesthetic disagreements will certainly be much smaller than would appear at a glance; and since no one really knows either how many relevant disagreements there really are, or how many would be too many, there is no evidence yet available to suggest that the number of aesthetic disagreements is incompatible with the objectivity of aesthetic terms.

But let us end here on a note of caution rather than triumph. The notion of "aesthetic term" has perhaps been treated in this place, and elsewhere, much too cavalierly, as if it were far more clear than it really is what terms belong under that head. Some have said that aesthetic terms can be identified with taste-terms; yet, as we have seen, there are terms which, on first reflection at least, we are willing to call aesthetic, but reluctant to call taste-terms. Others have said that all aesthetic terms are value-tending,[35] that is, counting either for or against the goodness or badness of the work of art. But although it is certainly true that some, like "unified" and "garish," are indeed unequivocally value-tending, others, "sentimental," for example, can sometimes count for, sometimes against the goodness of a work of art.[36] And, more important, emotive terms like "sad," "cheerful," "anguished," etc., which are claimed to be aesthetic and taste-terms, seem not, by themselves, to be value-tending at all. A work of art that is "unified" has a mark in its favor, whatever else it may be: but not a work that is "sad." Certainly it is clear that being "sad" sometimes is a mark of merit: if, for example the libretto calls for a "sad" aria to open the second act, or the composer has called his composition "Tragic Overture," then sadness will be a good-making feature of the aria or overture. But if, on the other hand, the libretto calls for a "cheerful" aria, or the composer has called his composition "Awakening of happy feelings on getting out into the country," sadness will be a bad-making feature. Finally, if the opening movement of a composition called "String Quartet, Opus 18, No. 4" happens to be "sad," it is difficult to see how the sadness is either a good- *or* a bad-making feature.

In these respects, then, the terms which writers have called "aesthetic" seem to be a mixed bag: some taste-terms, some not; some value-tending, some not. And this might well lead us to suspect at least that in another important respect, namely their logical behavior, aesthetic terms may be motley as well. Thus the only safe conclusion that can be reached here is that *some* aesthetic terms are certainly condition-governed, and some of the arguments used to demonstrate the non-condition-governed behavior of *all* aesthetic terms are bad arguments.

But the above conclusion is, I think, an important one in that it

[35] See, for example, Marcia P. Freedman, "The Myth of the Aesthetic Predicate," *Journal of Aesthetics and Art Criticism*, XXVII (1968).
[36] Cf. Dorothy Walsh, "Aesthetic Descriptions," *The British Journal of Aesthetics*, X (1970).

points out to us a philosophical dead-end which we should extricate ourselves from without delay. The distinction between the aesthetic and the nonaesthetic is a philosophical distinction of some interest; and the thesis that aesthetic terms are non-condition-governed is, at least implicitly, an attempt to draw that distinction along linguistic lines. It has failed on two counts: failed to show that all (or any) aesthetic terms are non-condition-governed and by this failure it has failed, as well, to give any encouragement to those who believe a line between the aesthetic and the nonaesthetic *can* be drawn by means of some distinctive linguistic behavior of aesthetic terms.

I do not mean to say that further investigation of the linguistic behavior of aesthetic terms would be worthless or uninteresting: quite to the contrary. But that it will yield a viable distinction between the aesthetic and nonaesthetic (if such a distinction really exists) seems very doubtful. The investigation, as Sibley has observed, "will be nasty, tedious and long."[37] And if the game is worth the candle, it is not going to be worth the candle it was once thought to be.

[37] Eva Schaper and Frank Sibley, "Symposium: About Taste," *The British Journal of Aesthetics*, VI (1966), p. 60.

BIBLIOGRAPHY OF WORKS CITED

Aldrich, Virgil C. *Philosophy of Art*. Englewood Cliffs, New Jersey: Prentice-Hall, 1963.
Apel, Willi. *The Harvard Dictionary of Music*. Cambridge, Massachusetts: Harvard University Press, 1951.
Austin, J. L. "A Plea for Excuses,"*Proceedings of the Aristotelian Society*, LVII (1956–57).
— *Philosophical Papers*. Edited by J. O. Urmson and G. J. Warnock. London: Oxford University Press, 1961.
— *Sense and Sensibilia*. Edited by G. J. Warnock. New York: Oxford University Press, 1964.
Bacon, Francis. *The Advancement of Learning*. London, 1605.
— "Of Beauty," *Essays, Advancement of Learning, New Atlantis, and Other Pieces*. Edited by R. F. Jones. New York: Odyssey Press, 1937.
Blom, Eric. *Mozart*. London: J. M. Dent, 1952.
Bouhours, Dominique. *Entretiens d'Ariste et d'Eugènie*. Amsterdam, 1671.
Brandt, Richard B. *Ethical Theory*. Englewood Cliffs, New Jersey: Prentice-Hall, 1959.
Burke, Edmund. *A Philosophical Enquiry into the Origin of our Ideas of the Sublime and Beautiful*. Edited by J. T. Boulton. New York: Columbia University Press, 1958.
Butler, Joseph. *Five Sermons*. New York: The Liberal Arts Press, 1950
Cavell, Marcia. "Critical Dialogue," *The Journal of Philosophy*, LXVII (1970).
Cohen, Marshall. "Appearance and the Aesthetic Attitude," *The Journal of Philosophy*, LVI (1959).
Duncan, Elmer H. "Arguments Used in Ethics and Aesthetics: Two Differences," *Journal of Aesthetics and Art Criticism*, XXV (1967).
Elledge, Scott, and Schier, Donald (eds.). *The Continental Model*. Minneapolis, Minnesota: University of Minnesota Press, 1960.
Freedman, Marcia P. "The Myth of the Aesthetic Predicate," *Journal of Aesthetics and Art Criticism*, XXVII (1968).
Gombrich, E. H. *Art and Illusion*. 2nd ed. New York: Pantheon Books, 1965.
— *The Story of Art*. London: Phaidon Press, 1952.
Goodman, Nelson. *Languages of Art*. New York: Bobbs-Merrill, 1968.
Grice, H. P. "The Causal Theory of Perception," *Proceedings of the Aristotelian Society*, Supplementary Volume, XXXV (1961).
Grove, George. *Beethoven and His Nine Symphonies*. New York: Dover Publications, 1962.
Gurney, Edmund. *The Power of Sound*. London: Smith, Elder, and Co., 1880.

Hanslick, Eduard. *The Beautiful in Music*. Translated by Gustav Cohen. New York: The Liberal Arts Press, 1957.

Hartshorne, Charles. *Philosophy and Psychology of Sensation*. Chicago: University of Chicago Press, 1934.

Hume, David. *Of the Standard of Taste, and Other Essays*. Edited by John Lenz. New York: Bobbs-Merrill, 1965.

Hungerland, Isabel C. "The Logic of Aesthetic Concepts," *Proceedings and Addresses of the American Philosophical Association*, XXXVI (1962–63).

Hutcheson, Francis. *An Inquiry into the Original of our Ideas of Beauty and Virtue*. 2nd ed. London, 1726.

Kant, Immanuel. *Critique of Aesthetic Judgement*. Translated by J. C. Meredith. London: Oxford University Press, 1911.

Kivy, Peter. "Aesthetic Aspects and Aesthetic Qualities," *The Journal of Philosophy*, LXV (1968).

— "Hume's Standard of Taste: Breaking the Circle," *The British Journal of Aesthetics*, VII (1967).

LaDrière, Craig. "The Problem of Plato's *Ion*," *Journal of Aesthetics and Art Criticism*, X (1951).

Lang, Paul Henry. *Music in Western Civilization*. New York: W. W. Norton, 1941.

Levin, David Michael. "More Aspects to the Concept of 'Aesthetic Aspects,'" *The Journal of Philosophy*, LXV (1968).

Mabbot, J. D. "Freewill and Punishment," *Contemporary British Philosophy*. Third Series. Edited by H. D. Lewis. London: George Allen and Unwin; New York: Macmillan, 1961.

Margolis, Joseph (ed.). *Philosophy Looks at the Arts*. New York: Charles Scribner's Sons, 1962.

Margolis, Joseph. "Sibley on Aesthetic Perception," *Journal of Aesthetics and Art Criticism*, XXV (1966).

Marliave, Joseph de. *Beethoven's Quartets*. Translated by Hilda Andrews. New York: Dover Publications, 1961.

Meynell, Hugo. "On the Foundations of Aesthetics," *The British Journal of Aesthetics*, VIII (1968).

Moore, G. E. *Ethics*. London: Oxford University Press, 1958.

Osborne, Harold. "Artistic Unity and Gestalt," *The Philosophical Quarterly*, XIV (1964).

— "On Artistic Illusion," *The British Journal of Aesthetics*, IX (1969)

— "Wittgenstein on Aesthetics," *The British Journal of Aesthetics*, VI (1966).

Plato. *Ion*. Translated by W. R. M. Lamb. Cambridge, Massachusetts and London: The Loeb Classical Library, 1962.

— *The Republic*. Translated by F. M. Cornford. New York and London: Oxford University Press, 1960.

Puttenham, George. *The Arte of English Poesie*. London, 1589.

Reynolds, Joshua. *Discourses*. Edited by Edmund Gosse. London: Kegan Paul, Trench, and Co., 1883.

Santayana, George. *The Sense of Beauty*. New York: Random House, 1955.

Schaper, Eva, and Sibley, Frank. "Symposium: About Taste," *The British Journal of Aesthetics*, VI (1966).

Sargeant, Winthrop. Music Reviews, *The New Yorker*, XLV (1969).

Sibley, Frank. "Aesthetic and Nonaestehtic," *The Philosophical Review*, LXXIV (1965).

— "Aesthetics and the Looks of Things," *The Journal of Philosophy*, LVI (1959).

— "Aesthetic Concepts," *The Philosophical Review*, LXVIII (1959).

— "Aesthetic Concepts: A Rejoinder," *The Philosophical Review*, LXXII (1963).
Sibley, F. N., and Tanner, Michael. "Objectivity and Aesthetics," *Proceedings of the Aristotelian Society*, Supplementary Volume, LXII (1968).
Sidney, Philip. *An Apologie for Poetrie*. London, 1595.
Smith, G. Gregory (ed.). *Elizabethan Critical Essays*. 2 vols. London: Oxford University Press, 1904.
Spingarn, J. E. (ed.). *Critical Essays of the Seventeenth Century*. 3 vols. London: Oxford University Press, 1957.
Stampp, Kenneth M. "Unity as a Necessary Condition," *Journal of Aesthetics and Art Criticism*, XXVII (1968).
Stebbing, L. Susan. *Philosophy and the Physicists*. New York: Dover Publications 1958.
Stolnitz, Jerome. "On the Origins of 'Aesthetic Disinterestedness,'" *Journal of Aesthetics and Art Criticism*, XX (1961).
Strawson, P. F. Review of Harold Osborne's *Theory of Beauty*, *Mind*, New Series, LXIII (1954).
Swartz, Robert J. (ed.). *Perceiving, Sensing, and Knowing*. Garden City, New York: Doubleday Anchor Books, 1965.
Tilghman, B. R. "Aesthetic Perception and the Problem of the 'Aesthetic Object,'" *Mind*, New Series, LXXV (1966).
— *The Expression of Emotion in the Visual Arts: A Philosophical Inquiry*. The Hague: Martinus Nijhoff, 1970.
Tomas, Vincent. "Aesthetic Vision," *The Philosophical Review*, LXVIII (1959).
— "The Concept of Expression in Art," *Science, Language, and Human Rights*. Philadelphia: University of Pennsylvania Press, 1952.
Toulmin, Stephen. *Reason in Ethics*. Cambridge University Press, 1968.
Tovey, Donald Francis. *Essays in Musical Analysis*. 6 vols. London: Oxford University Press, 1935–39.
Urmson, J. O. *The Emotive Theory of Ethics*. New York: Oxford University Press, 1969.
Walsh, Dorothy. "Aesthetic Descriptions," *The British Journal of Aesthetics*, X (1970).
Warrack, John. *Carl Maria von Weber*. New York: Macmillan, 1968.
Weitz, Morris. "The Role of Theory in Aesthetics," *Journal of Aesthetics and Art Criticism*, XV (1956).
Williamson, J. Review of Joseph Margolis' *Philosophy Looks at the Arts*, *Australasian Journal of Philosophy*, XLI (1963).
Wisdom, John. "Metaphysics and Verification," *Mind*, New Series, XLVII (1938).
— *Philosophy and Psychoanalysis*. Oxford: Basil Blackwell, 1964.
Wittgenstein, Ludwig. *The Blue and Brown Books*. New York: Harper Torchbooks, 1965.
— *Philosophical Investigations*. Translated by G. E. M. Anscombe. New York: Macmillan, 1953.
Wollheim, Richard. *Art and Its Objects: An Introduction to Aesthetics*. New York: Harper and Row, 1968.

INDEX

Addison, Joseph, 111
aesthetic (and nonasesthetic), 38, 94–95, 129
aesthetic appreciation, 90–92
aesthetic approval, 17
aesthetic attitude, 71–72, 82
aesthetic contemplation, 38
aesthetic descriptions, 43, 48–50
aesthetic disagreements
    attitude towards, 117–121,127
    extent of, 121–127
aesthetic discourse, 117–127
aesthetic disinterestedness, 70–72
aesthetic excellence, 94
aesthetic experience, 38, 90–92
aesthetic hearing, 74–75
aesthetic perception, 37–38, 70–72, 87, 89–96, 111
aesthetic point of view, 37, 78–82
aesthetic psychology, 111
aesthetic sensitivity, *see* taste
aesthetic terms
    and aesthetic disagreements, 117–127
    and aesthetic vision, 70–83
    and aspect-ascribing, 96–106
    and aspect-perceiving, 87–106
    and common sense, 108
    and condition-governing, 41–50
    and emotive terms, 128
    and new cases, 50–55
    and nonaesthetic terms, 36–40
    and objective qualities, 114–117, 127
    and Plato, 111
    and Platonism, 113
    and seems-is distinction, 61–70
    and taste, 56–60
    and taste-terms, 36–40, 128
    and value-tending terms, 128
aesthetic vision, 72–83, 111, 113
Aldrich, Virgil C., 93–94
Andrews, Hilda, 5n
Anscombe, G. E. M., 86n
"antinomy of taste," 118

Apel, Willi, 38n
appearance, 73–82, 93–94
appearance and reality, 61–83, 111–114, 116
appreciation, 57–60
aspect-ascribing, 96–106
aspect-perceiving, 87–106
Austin, J. L., 68–69, 89

Bach, J. S., 19–20, 25, 33–34, 52
Bacon, Francis, 110
beauty (and ugliness), 26–27
Beethoven, Ludwig van, 5, 7, 9, 19, 33–34, 92
being and appearing, 6–17. *See also* appearance and reality, and seems-is distinction
Berkeley, George, 108
Blom, Eric, 53n
Bouhours, Dominique, 26
Boulton, J. T., 71n
Brahms, Johannes, 18, 20
Brandt, R. B., 123n
Brubeck, Stan, 10
Bruckner, Anton, 15–16
Budge, Don, 35
Burke, Edmund, 71–72
Butler, Joseph, 9n

Caligula, 27
Cavell, Marcia, 115n
Christmas Oratorio (Bach), 20
Cohen, Gustav, 124n
Cohen, Marshall, 74
color terms, 63–68
common sense (aesthetic), 108, 114, 127
condition-governed terms
    and appearance, 37–38
    and aspect-ascribing, 96–106
    and aspect-perceiving, 87–106
    and common sense, 108
    and descriptions, 43–50
    and evaluation, 45–46